"This is a book every Christian [masterful guide through an emotional and theological minefield, full of wisdom and compassion, scripturally sound, and eminently practical. *Critical Conversations* fills a critically important void."

—Dr. Michael L. Brown, author of *Can You Be Gay and Christian?* and host of The Line of Fire radio broadcast

"In this age of gender confusion and ethical license, it is more important than ever that Christian families uphold scriptural standards regarding sexuality and morality. Tom Gilson speaks to these issues with valuable insight in *Critical Conversations: A Christian Parents' Guide to Discussing Homosexuality with Teens.* We are now ministering in a time when many professed Christians appear predisposed against God's standards—and this is especially true among youth, which is why *Critical Conversations* is such an important resource for every church and Christian home. A veteran apologist and ministry strategist who delivers realistic plans for imparting biblical truth to this generation, Tom Gilson is one writer whose insights I never miss—and this may just be his most significant work ever."

—Alex McFarland, director for Christian Worldview and Apologetics, North Greenville University, Tigerville, South Carolina

"*Critical Conversations* helps Christian parents tell the truth about homosexuality in a compassionate manner. It does so for the sake of equipping young believers to do the same. Can there be a more important task in our world where many of our friends and family members identify as gay and lesbian? Simply put, if you have children, you need to read this book."

—Alan Shlemon, author and speaker for Stand to Reason

"Homosexuality and same-sex 'marriage' have dominated the headlines, and anyone with children knows the relentless propaganda young people are subject to on these issues. There are many fine books describing the perils of same-sex 'marriage' and defending natural marriage from its critics. Tom Gilson's book is unique: it provides thoughtful, concise ways to explain these issues to our children. If you have children, you owe it to them to read this book."

—Jay W. Richards, PhD, author and assistant research professor, The Catholic University of America, Washington, DC

CRITICAL CONVERSATIONS

A Christian Parents' Guide
to Discussing Homosexuality
with TEENS

TOM GILSON

Foreword by Sean McDowell

Kregel
Publications

Critical Conversations: A Christian Parents' Guide to Discussing Homosexuality with Teens
© 2016 by Tom Gilson

Published by Kregel Publications, a division of Kregel, Inc., 2450 Oak Industrial Drive NE, Grand Rapids, MI 49505.

The authors and publisher are not engaged in rendering medical or psychological services, and this book is not intended as a guide to diagnose or treat medical or psychological problems. If medical, psychological, or other expert assistance is required, the reader should seek the services of a health care provider or certified counselor.

Scripture quotations are from The Holy Bible, English Standard Version® (ESV®), copyright © 2001 by Crossway, a publishing ministry of Good News Publishers. Used by permission. All rights reserved.

ISBN 978-0-8254-4396-1

Printed in the United States of America

16 17 18 19 20 21 22 23 24 25 / 5 4 3 2 1

To my marvelous wife, Sara, with whom and from whom I learned most of what I have come to know about parenting, and to Jonathan and Lisa, our children, who have made it through the teenage years with a strong faith in Christ. May God continue to bless them with solid belief in Christ and the ability to stand strong amid all the challenges they're facing that their parents never had to.

CONTENTS

FOREWORD

Sean McDowell

As parents, my wife and I have many difficult conversations with our kids. Some conversations are a natural part of parenting, and others arise because of the age we live in. Homosexuality is an example of the latter. While parents have always needed to talk to their kids about sex, the need to talk about homosexuality is relatively new.

Whether or not we want to acknowledge it, here's the reality: *our kids are growing up in a world where homosexual behavior is viewed as normal and praiseworthy.* In fact, those who question the morality of homosexual behavior are considered hateful bigots. Homosexuality depicted as a positive lifestyle choice is everywhere—television, schools, the news, Hollywood, the Internet, and even many churches. If you think homosexual behavior is wrong, then *you*, culturally speaking, are the problem.

As Christian parents, how should we respond? Should we avoid the subject? Should we really have this conversation with our kids? If so, when? And what should we say? How do we answer their tough questions? How do we teach our kids to respond both lovingly and biblically to this pressing issue?

If you are a parent, you no doubt wrestle with these questions. You want to speak truth, and you want to speak it in love. While there are no easy answers to the many difficult issues that arise surrounding the topic of homosexuality, I am grateful Tom has written *Critical Conversations*. As a parent myself, and as a youth worker, I found his book immensely helpful. Here are three things I appreciate about it.

First, *Critical Conversations* is compassionate. Tom clearly holds the traditional view on human sexuality. He believes that sex is to be experienced in marriage, which he rightly views as a permanent, exclusive union between one man and one woman. And yet Tom is gracious toward those who hold different views. He does not disparage his opponents nor does he set up straw men. His tone is a breath of fresh air.

Second, *Critical Conversations* is well researched. Tom has done his homework! It is clear that Tom is widely read on the issue and weighs in as an expert.

Third, *Critical Conversations* is practical. While the whole book is insightful and important, part 3 is particularly practical. Tom briefly responds to the most common challenges teens often raise against the historic Christian view of sex and marriage. Tom will equip you with the knowledge and confidence to graciously handle the toughest questions your teens may ask.

It is easy to avoid tough issues because we are afraid of how our teens may respond. But this is a topic we simply cannot avoid. If we don't talk to our teens about homosexuality and help them to see God's loving design, they will inevitably adopt the views of the culture we live in. While this book certainly doesn't answer every question related to the topic (what book does?), it will give you a road map for helping teens address a critical issue of our day. And it will help you do it with kindness and gentleness (see 1 Peter 3:15).

Sean McDowell, PhD, is a professor at Biola University, an internationally acclaimed speaker, and best-selling author of over fifteen books including *A New Kind of Apologist*. He blogs regularly at SeanMcDowell.org.

PREFACE

June 26, 2015. Everything changed—and nothing changed.

Everything changed. With the stroke of a pen on that day, the US Supreme Court legalized same-sex marriage, ending years of legal disputes, political campaigns, and legislative and judicial maneuverings. The court settled the matter.

Nothing changed. The legal questions may have been settled (at least for now), but the moral and spiritual questions haven't been, and they're not going away anytime soon. Christianity still has the same reputation for opposing gay rights. We're standing for the truth of God as revealed in Scripture and in nature, holding on as best we can to the true meaning of marriage and morality. But we're viewed as anti-gay, anti-equality bigots, stuck in the past, trying to foist a bronze-age morality on the rest of the world.

Our teens know where we stand. For them it's an incredibly uncomfortable place to be, but we know it's a good place, a place of truth: the place God intended for us all to stand.

American Christians face challenges today unlike any we've encountered before. Our teens in particular are surrounded by pro–lesbian, gay, bisexual, and transgender (LGBT) messages. (Almost all of this applies to preteens, too, but for simplicity I'll only refer to teens in this book.) Their friends overwhelmingly support gay-rights causes. There's an almost perfect storm of awkward parent-child topics to be found here: sex, relationships, peer pressure, generational differences, and our own sense of being poorly informed and ill-equipped for the conversation. To be opposed to homosexuality is to be old and out of touch.

My wife and I have been through these issues with our son and daughter. We didn't do everything right with them, but we're grateful to be able to say that they both still share our beliefs as young adults now. Both of them also paid the price for it—especially our daughter, who was bullied frequently for her Christian convictions.

As tough as our kids' experiences as believers were, though, it would have been far worse if we had abandoned them to a culture gone crazy. We knew that God expected far more from us as parents than that. We knew how much our children's lives, health, and spiritual well-being depended on our training them in the fear and admonition of the Lord.

I believe you share that knowledge and conviction. I believe you want your children to grow up affirming the timeless truths of Christ, including God's teachings on marriage and morality, whether reaching that goal is easy or hard. You just want some guidance in how best to prepare your children in those truths. That's what this book is for.

I'm sure that talking with your teenage child about homosexuality sounds hard to do, but here's the good news: it doesn't have to be nearly as awkward or difficult as you might think. You can do it. All it takes is some preparation. You can learn to understand the basic issues behind gay activism. You can become familiar with what the Bible really says about homosexuality and how human experience supports what the Bible teaches. You can use relational parenting principles that will help make your conversations with your kids on this topic seem natural, not weird.

My prayer is that you'll have these critical conversations, and that your relationship with your teen will grow through the experience. Most of all, I pray that your teen will gain the knowledge and strength to stand with the Word of God and keep growing in Christ, no matter what he or she might face.

Tom Gilson
Lebanon, Ohio
July 2015

If you need to talk with your teen about questions he or she has about his or her own sexual orientation or gender identity, I pray you will find a competent and caring Christian counselor nearby to help you and your family members. This book does not tackle that difficult and sensitive matter.

CHAPTER ONE
Introduction

Bigot. Hater. Intolerant. Christian.

Christians were rarely labeled that way when I was growing up. We sure are today. The gay marriage movement has branded Christianity with that image, they've branded you and me with it, and, worst of all, they've stuck those labels on our Christian sons and daughters. To be a committed, believing Christian in today's world, especially the world our youth live in, is to be considered an intolerant bigot.

On television, in the classrooms, in political debates, in music and film, and all over the Internet, the message is relentlessly repeated: *If you're a Christian, you're a hater.* Christian young people have too few places of refuge from that cutting criticism. They can't help wondering, *If that's what it means to be a Christian, do I want it?*

Many teens answer that question with a no. Although survey results differ in their details, all researchers agree that at least half of all youth brought up in Christian homes will walk away from the faith when they leave home for college or career.[1] Some studies indicate that as many as three-quarters of Christian youth abandon the

---

1. For a single source compiling the best of such research in one place, see Stephen Cable, *Cultural Captives: The Beliefs and Behavior of American Young Adults* (Plano, TX: Probe Ministries, 2013).

faith. These are our children. They're teens who come out of strong evangelical homes and churches. They could be your children.

My wife and I have a twenty-four-year-old son and a twenty-year-old daughter. They used to ask us for help with their homework. They asked us about math or geography or science—questions they were expecting to face on tests at school. There was another test they faced regularly, though it never showed up in a class syllabus or agenda. Every student in public school faces this test at least weekly, and every student who listens to music, watches TV or films, or surfs the Internet does, too. This test has items like,

Why can't gays get married?

Who says gay sex is wrong?

I heard someone say the Bible doesn't really teach there's anything wrong with homosexuality.

What about the two men sharing the house down the street? They're great people. I don't see anything wrong with them—doesn't their relationship count, too?

And on it goes. If you haven't heard your teens asking questions like these, it isn't because they're not being tested on them. On Facebook and on film, on the school bus and in the lunchroom, these challenges are unavoidable.

The Turning of the Tide

Can you believe how quickly the world has changed? Today's teens face moral pressures that never entered our minds, and they're navigating relationship complications that never invaded our nightmares. When our daughter, Lisa, was in ninth grade, she told us about having a female friend she liked a lot—and then she quickly interjected, "But not like *that*, you know." I had great same-sex friends in high school, but I never had to say to my parents, "But not like *that*." Even that disclaimer has become morally suspect. On television it would almost certainly be followed by the iconic Seinfeld line, "Not that there's anything wrong with it."

Same-sex couples kissed on the cover of *Time* on April 8, 2013; transgenderism made the June 9, 2014, cover; and in June 2015 the US

Supreme Court ruled that gay marriage should be considered right, proper, and normal. Bruce/Caitlyn Jenner's photo appeared on the cover of *Vanity Fair* shortly after that, and ESPN honored him/her like a hero for it.[2] We've descended to the level where immorality is no longer a matter just of practice but of hearty approval (Rom. 1:32). Our children face a tough choice: they can deny Scripture and, arguably, common sense, to chime in with culture and voice their own approval for deep wrongs; or they can take a positive, biblically moral stance, no matter what their friends, teachers, and the media say.

Signed Up for the Job

I'll bet you don't remember signing up for this when you became a parent. You've got the job anyway. Maybe you're banking on your church covering these hard topics for you and your family (and honestly I hope you would be right about that), but most churches aren't taking up the challenge, and even fewer are doing a good job of it. (Your pastor or youth leader might find this book helpful, by the way.)

Even if your church is one of the few that's teaching youth about this, you're still the parent. No one else can match your impact on your child's long-term spiritual health. The Bible makes your responsibility quite clear. Deuteronomy 6:1–7 says,

> Now this is the commandment—the statutes and the rules—that the LORD your God commanded me to teach you, that you may do them in the land to which you are going over, to possess it, that you may fear the LORD your God, you and your son and your son's son, by keeping all his statutes and his commandments, which I command you, all the days of your life, and that your days may be long. Hear therefore, O Israel, and be careful to do them, that it may go well with you, and that you may multiply greatly, as the LORD, the God of

---

2. "Caitlyn Jenner vows to 'reshape the landscape' in ESPYS speech," ESPN.com news service, July 16, 2015, espn.go.com/espys/2015/story/_/id/13264599/caitlyn -jenner-accepts-arthur-ashe-courage-award-espys-ashe2015.

your fathers, has promised you, in a land flowing with milk and honey.

Hear, O Israel: The LORD our God, the LORD is one. You shall love the LORD your God with all your heart and with all your soul and with all your might. And these words that I command you today shall be on your heart. You shall teach them diligently to your children, and shall talk of them when you sit in your house, and when you walk by the way, and when you lie down, and when you rise.

There's no guaranteed formula for keeping children spiritually strong, wise, and faithful, but the Bible and experience both indicate that parents' involvement is the number one factor in children's lifelong faith and spiritual development. The National Study on Youth and Religion, a long-term research program led by Christian Smith, has been following several thousand American young people from their teen years into early adulthood, exploring almost every facet of their spiritual, social, and academic lives. His team's findings on young adults are strikingly consistent. Of course every child is different, and group trends don't tell individual stories. Still it's clear that the path we want our children to follow—from church-attending youth to spiritually alive young adult—almost always involves parents with strong faith freely expressed in the family setting. Conversely, the path from highly religious teens to least religious adults virtually always includes spiritually uninvolved parents.[3]

This isn't just about taking your kids to church with you and praying before meals. It's about interaction. The Fuller Youth Institute conducted research on what makes faith stick. (It's reported in a family-friendly way in *Sticky Faith: Everyday Ideas to Build Lasting Faith in Your Kids* by Dr. Kara E. Powell and Dr. Chap Clark.)[4] The authors tell us "the core of Sticky Faith is developing a clear and honest understanding of

3. Christian Smith with Patricia Snell, *Souls in Transition: The Religious and Spiritual Lives of Emerging Adults* (New York: Oxford University Press, 2009).

4. Kara E. Powell and Chap Clark, *Sticky Faith: Everyday Ideas to Build Lasting Faith in Your Kids* (Grand Rapids: Zondervan, 2011).

both the gospel and biblical faith" in students.[5] That makes sense; but where will that understanding come from? Very few gain it from their parents. Powell and Clark cite research showing that only "12 percent of [churched] youth have a regular dialogue with their mom on faith or life issues. . . . It's far lower for dads. One out of twenty kids, or 5 percent, has regular faith or life conversations with their dad. . . . When it comes to matters of faith, mum's the word at home."[6]

Powell and Clark found that when parents have honest and transparent conversations with their children about faith, kids typically come out stronger in the long run. That's a clear teaching of the Bible, and it's well supported by experience. Why then do so few parents take the initiative?

Obstacles Parents Face

I suspect there are three main reasons parents don't have more faith conversations with their children, much less deep discussions on tough topics like homosexuality. I'll start with the easy one first.

1. We don't have time to talk. I can guess what you're thinking right now: *If that's the easy reason, what are the hard ones? We never have time to talk!* Here's the thing, though: faith conversations don't need to be long sit-down sessions—indeed, most of the time they shouldn't be.

In our family we've done it both poorly and well. What's worked best has been a mix of methods: quick grab-and-go conversations while the kids are getting ready in the morning or while we're driving them to school, along with longer discussions once in a while over meals. Simply making faith conversations a part of the routine can go a long way. Powell and Clark offer pages of great suggestions along these lines in *Sticky Faith.*

2. We're not sure what to say. Faith questions can be tough, and, these days, the ones we're working on in this book are probably the hardest

---

5. Ibid., 22.
6. Ibid., 46–47.

of all. I'm confident you'll find *Critical Conversations* to be helpful in preparing you for these conversations. It might even prepare you (see chapter 7) for a big win with your teen when you least expect it: when you don't have an answer to what they're asking.

3. We're stuck on hold. Face it: some conversations are hard to start. We're unsure of ourselves. We have history with our teens, too. In our mind's eye we can see them rolling their eyes at us even before we get started. We see the discussion turning into a lecture (from our teen's point of view, at any rate) and then into a fight.

That's certainly one way it could go. Still, most children would jump at the chance to have their parents take their difficult questions seriously. If our teens don't seem interested, it might be that they don't sense we're treating them or the questions seriously.

I've found that if I'll watch a show with my kids, I can talk with them about its spiritual implications. Or if I take one of them out for breakfast or lunch, they'll tell me (eventually) what's on their minds. As we're heading out they might wonder out loud, "Is this going to be one of those talks?" And of course, if it's "one of those talks" every time we go out, that's counterproductive. We need to do fun things together without an agenda, too. But they do love it when they find out their dad cares for them enough to have a serious conversation with them about serious topics.

How To Use This Book

This book is meant to help you as a parent, and it does so in a way that's different from most others you've read. It's divided into two distinct sections. Parts 1 and 2, chapters 2 through 8, are organized the way most books usually are, with chapter-length discussions on major topics. Part 3 is where *Critical Conversations* is unique. It may be unlike anything you've seen in any other parenting book. It's filled with brief, intensely practical *Wow-I-could-use-this-right-now!* sorts of information. (I'll say more about part 3 shortly.)

Here's an overview of the whole book. First, since it's important to get a broad perspective on these topics (otherwise the specific details make little sense), part 1, chapters 2 through 4, sets forth that big-picture view of the LGBT controversy.

This introduction is chapter 1. Chapter 2 describes the lay of the land, revealing how gay-rights activists took advantage of weaknesses in Western culture's moral structure to manipulate us into the strange conflict we are now in, leading to their decisive win on gay marriage.

In chapters 3 and 4, I examine the biblical case for *natural marriage* (marriage between a man and a woman) and the standards of sexual morality that have ruled Western culture for centuries—in theory, that is, if not always in practice. I include support from other sources along with the Bible. After all, while Scripture is persuasive to those of us who know that it's the true Word of God, others often regard it as little better than "a bronze-age book of fables."[7] For that reason these chapters include information to explain *why* God's commands are good—in terms that can help you explain it to nonbelievers as well as believers.

In part 2, chapters 5 through 8, I reflect on parents' and teens' relationships from multiple angles. Chapter 5 speaks of keeping God our number one life priority in all truth, wisdom, humility, and conviction. Chapter 6 deals with our relationships with our teens, with helpful principles for keeping conversations healthy and productive, even on a hot topic like this one. Chapter 7 offers guidance you can give your teens regarding the way they relate with their LGBT or pro-LGBT friends and classmates. Chapter 8 covers territory having to do with their teachers and school administrators—not only how your teens can best deal with them, but also how you can best relate with those authority figures in your child's life.

Finally, part 3—a section unlike any you've probably seen before— examines how Christians can defend our beliefs confidently and winsomely in the face of twenty-seven anti-Christian gay-rights slogans, stingers, and other common challenges. These are short,

---

7. This is a frequent Internet meme that can be found in abundance by searching for "Bronze Age collection fables Bible."

pithy kinds of messages of the sort that our teens encounter every-where: on bumper stickers, billboards, buttons, placards, posters, and of course Twitter, Facebook, and other media. These challenges can seem powerful: they elicit strong emotional responses, they call forth our sense of justice, and they speak to our core values of "life, liberty, and the pursuit of happiness." Or at least on the surface they do; what's behind the message isn't always what it first appears to be.

Each topic in part 3 (they're too short to be called *chapters*) presents a moment's worth of informed thought, focused on one particular message, to give you a tool rack of ready questions and answers to discuss together with your teens.

These topics are brief and completely modular. You can read through them in sequence, you can skip around from topic to topic, or you can simply keep them handy as reference material for when a particular issue comes up. Before you dive into any of them, though, please be sure to read the introduction to part 3 beginning on page 96. It has crucial information on how to use that part of the book, especially "Tips for Talking with Your Teen."

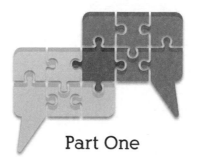

Part One

ESSENTIAL BACKGROUND

CHAPTER TWO
How Did We Get Here?

What hit us?

Have you wondered about that? I know I have. Others have, too. Matthew J. Franck, an attorney with the Alliance Defending Freedom, tells about hearing a pair of professors, both of them at least seventy years old, holding forth on the supposedly obvious justice of same-sex marriage. Something struck him as "remarkable," he says.

> Both gentlemen expressed the opinion that the cause of same-sex marriage was obviously just, that opponents of the cause were obviously reactionary and benighted, and that this was plainly the new civil rights struggle of our time.
>
> Yet it struck me that if denying same-sex couples the "right to marry" was such an obvious and gross injustice as to merit such energetic claims today, why had it never occurred to either of these august scholars decades ago, at the beginning or the middle of their careers? In the books of proud advocacy each had published, say, twenty or thirty years ago, there was not the slightest hint that American public life was disfigured by this particular injustice.
>
> Redefining marriage to include same-sex relationships simply didn't occur to them, because it didn't occur to anyone.

Yet that day they espoused that view with the fervor of men who had always thought so, and for whom it was unthinkable to believe otherwise.[1]

The article is titled "Same-Sex Marriage and Social Change: Exceeding the Speed of Thought." It's an apt title. What happened to make same-sex relationships so "obviously right" that the Supreme Court would legitimize them as marriage? How did Christians become "haters"? *And how did that happen so fast?*

The story isn't pleasant, but it's instructive. Gay-rights leaders haven't played nice in their campaign for social upheaval.

Setting the Stage

It goes back to the sexual revolution of the 1960s—a huge social upheaval that had virtually nothing at first to do with homosexuality, yet laid the foundation for all that's happened since. Today's gay-rights activism would have been literally unthinkable apart from the '60s. Popular media had long fueled the idea that romance and sexual expression were at the pinnacle of all human good, but it was in the '60s that young people really took that distorted message to heart. It was also the decade when sex became a matter of recreation, disconnected (mostly through contraception) from childbearing, and thus also from marriage.

Once there was a time—it's almost hard to remember now—when sex and childbearing were tightly linked to one another. Couples sharing intimacy couldn't ignore the possibility of children, so sex was always about "the two of us, and the kids we can expect to come along after sharing this kind of intimacy." The pill changed that dramatically. Children could be eliminated from the equation, so for many people sex became a matter of "just you and me, babe."

That set the stage for a result that should have been obvious from

---

1. Matthew J. Franck, "Same-Sex Marriage and Social Change: Exceeding the Speed of Thought," *Public Discourse*, January 4, 2013, www.thepublicdiscourse.com/2013/01/7495/.

the outset. If sexuality is about "just you and me, babe," and if what matters in sex is what makes us happy for the moment, why limit sex to marriage? Why limit it to a man and a woman? *Why limit sex at all?* With sex supposedly having no consequences, biblical morality became just about the only restraint on it. Those who had disregarded biblical morality saw little reason to confine their sexual expression inside any boundaries at all.

Still, apart from a small number of gay activists with high hopes of changing the world, gay marriage was a long way from anyone's mind. Fast-forward a decade or two from there. Gay activists Marshall Kirk and "Erastes Pill" (a pseudonym used by Hunter Madsen) published an article in 1987 that we Christians should have paid more attention to. The title was forthright enough: "The Overhauling of Straight America."[2] A few years later they followed it with a book, *After the Ball: How America Will Conquer Its Fear and Hatred of Gays in the 90's.* It's an impressive piece of writing, in a way: it's one of the most disturbingly brilliant works of strategy I have ever read. The authors knew how to make change happen. And change has indeed happened—at the "speed of thought," to borrow Matthew Franck's words.

Commentators typically place the beginning of the gay-rights movement at the 1969 Stonewall Riots in New York City, a reaction to an early morning police raid on a gay bar called the Stonewall Inn. Gay activism was powerfully evident just three years later at a meeting of the American Psychiatric Association. Militants disrupted the meeting, demanding that the APA declassify homosexuality as a mental disorder. As one of the participants described it, "Our presence there was only the beginning of an increasingly intensive campaign by homosexuals to change the approach of psychiatry toward homosexuality or, failing that, to discredit psychiatry."[3] The APA

---

2. Marshall Kirk and Erastes Pill, "The Overhauling of Straight America," accessed October 26, 2015, library.gayhomeland.org/0018/EN/EN_Overhauling_Straight .htm. This article appeared in *Guide Magazine*, November 1987.

3. Robert R. Reilly, *Making Gay Okay: How Rationalizing Homosexual Behavior Is Changing Everything* (San Francisco: Ignatius Press, 2014), 120. See chapter 7 of this book for a further description of events at this APA convention.

acquiesced—not, by the way, because of any new scientific information regarding the healthfulness of homosexuality.

I asked Michael Brown, author of one of the best analyses of the gay-rights movement I've seen, about the role Kirk and Madsen's work played in the history of LGBT activism.[4] Did their article and their book form gay-rights strategies or merely reflect strategies already in operation? His opinion was that it was probably something in between: the article and the book expressed what the movement's leaders were generally thinking, and they helped to focus those thoughts. Regardless, we should have paid more attention at the time, as you're about to see. I'll concentrate my discussion here on the shorter piece, "The Overhauling of Straight America."

How to Get Overhauled

In that article, Kirk and Madsen recommended six steps toward widespread acceptance of homosexuality.[5] Each of the steps was expanded upon in their article, naturally, yet their topic headings alone are enough to demonstrate the nature of the tactics they were prepared to put in motion:

1. Talk about gays and gayness as loudly and as often as possible. The principle behind this advice is simple: almost any behavior begins to look normal if you are exposed to enough of it at close quarters and among your acquaintances. . . .
2. Portray gays as victims, not as aggressive challengers. . . .
3. Give protectors [of gays] a just cause. . . .
4. Make gays look good. In order to make a Gay Victim sympathetic to straights you have to portray him as Everyman. . . . Paint gays as superior pillars of society. . . .
5. Make the victimizers look bad. . . .
6. Solicit funds: the bucks stop here.

---

4. See Michael L. Brown, *A Queer Thing Happened to America: And What a Long Strange Trip It's Been* (Concord, NC: EqualTime Books, 2011).
5. The following block quotes are all from Kirk and Pill, "The Overhauling of Straight America."

Point five deserves special attention, for it includes the following:

> Make the antigays look so nasty that average Americans will want to dissociate themselves from such types. The public should be shown images of ranting homophobes whose secondary traits and beliefs disgust middle America. These images might include: the Ku Klux Klan demanding that gays be burned alive or castrated; bigoted southern ministers drooling with hysterical hatred to a degree that looks both comical and deranged; menacing punks, thugs, and convicts speaking coolly about the "fags" they have killed or would like to kill; a tour of Nazi concentration camps where homosexuals were tortured and gassed.

Does that sound familiar? (I won't ask whether you think it sounds just or fair.) Further into the article, the authors make recommendations for mainstream media spots. Under the unfriendly heading of "Format E for Vilification of Victimizers" they say,

> These images [of ranting and hateful religious extremists, neo-Nazis, and Ku Klux Klansmen] should be combined with those of their gay victims by a method propagandists call the "bracket technique." For example, for a few seconds an unctuous beady-eyed Southern preacher is seen pounding the pulpit in rage about "those sick, abominable creatures." While his tirade continues over the soundtrack, the picture switches to pathetic photos of gays who look decent, harmless, and likable; and then we cut back to the poisonous face of the preacher, and so forth. The contrast speaks for itself. The effect is devastating.

Why do I tell you about this? Because it shows how thoroughly we've been manipulated. More to the point, it shows how *our children* have been manipulated. The "bracket technique," which Kirk and Madsen themselves described as propagandistic, had nothing to do with rational persuasion or moral reasoning. Their whole strategy was nothing but imagery and emotional engineering.

Their book *After the Ball* contains more of the same, along with an impassioned but self-serving plea that gay, lesbian, and transgender people downplay their nontraditional and flamboyant ways of dressing and acting. The idea was to begin gaining public acceptance, which meant putting a halt (for now) to doing things in public that shocked straight people or made them feel uncomfortable. Again, imagery was paramount; the goal was to present a face to the public that would evoke sympathy. Rather than a detestable and shameful sin, homosexuality was to be viewed as just another version of normal.

They had a plan. They carried it out. It worked. In retrospect, why should it seem so astonishing? And yet look at what they've accomplished:

> While people in the LGBT community were calculating ways to destroy Christians' reputations in the public mind, they managed to make it seem like *we* were the haters.
>
> While they were waging a highly aggressive campaign to change centuries of moral tradition, they managed to make us seem as if we were the aggressors.
>
> While they were making themselves seem to be the victims, they were victimizing conservatives, especially Christians.
>
> While they were seeking to make their sexuality acceptable in the scope of ordinary, normal human activity, they were dehumanizing their opponents.

Summary

This bit of history helps answer Matthew Franck's question about how two professors' opinions about "obvious" justice could have so completely morphed within a twenty-year span. It's largely because of propagandistic strategies like those in "The Overhauling of Straight America." More generally, it's because we lost our moral moorings, for we dare not forget the big picture: this isn't about straight people versus gay people. It's about a solid moral culture versus a shifting one. It wasn't LGBT people who led the way, it was straight culture's rejection of sexual morality. The LGBT movement has just been part of the consequence. Once a culture gives up its moral stability, there's no telling where or in what shape it's going to land.

Tuck that away in the back of your mind for now. It will help you understand not only what you and your kids have been experiencing, but also some of what follows as we continue through our discussion.

CHAPTER THREE

What Marriage Is

*"So God created man in his own image, in the image of
God he created him; male and female he created them."*
(Genesis 1:27)

Our identity is in God. He defines our nature. He created us male
and female. That's basic to this entire discussion, and it's at the heart
of what marriage is.

We have a lot to discuss concerning God and the nature of marriage. Before we go into that, though, I'd like to take a short yet
important detour through another crucial facet of who we are in the
sight of God.

Before Genesis 1:27 speaks of "male and female," it says we were
made "in his own image." In other words, before sex, before gender,
and before sexuality, there was the image of God in the people he
created. We're *all* made in God's image. We all have equal worth in
his eyes. If he views us all equally, then we ought to view one another
as equally worthy.

LGBT people have felt dehumanized by Christians. Granted,
they've done that partly to themselves by feeding themselves the same
ranting-preacher images they've fed the rest of the world. One reason

they believe Christians hate them is because they've been working overtime to convince themselves we do. They're victims of the errors in their own propaganda.

Still we need to ask ourselves, what makes those messages even remotely believable in the first place? There must be some kernel of reality to them.

And there is. Andrew Marin's book *Love Is an Orientation: Elevating the Conversation with the Gay Community* tells one heartbreaking story after another of LGBT people being hurt by Christians.[1] Probably the deepest hurt has been caused by Christians treating them as less than human: pushing them aside, making false assumptions, and doing so without actually bothering to get to know any of them.

In my relationships and in my own blogging on this subject, I have repeatedly issued a plea for us all to treat one another as human beings. I've made that plea in both directions. First, I've spoken it toward the LGBT community.[2] I don't appreciate the way conservative Christians have been "overhauled," and made out to be monsters and haters. I've said, "If you want to call me a hater, at least sit down and have a cup of coffee with me first. Find out who I really am. Treat me as a human being before you put labels on me, please—even though I know you disagree with me."[3]

Second, I've issued a similar plea to my fellow conservative Christians.[4] If we want to be treated as human beings, it's only right that we treat others as human beings—even if we disagree with them. The reason that's right isn't just because that's how we want

1. Andrew Marin, *Love Is an Orientation: Elevating the Conversation with the Gay Community* (Downers Grove, IL: IVP Books, 2009).

2. See, e.g., "To Treat One Another as Humans," Thinking Christian blog, November 28, 2010, www.thinkingchristian.net/posts/2010/11/to-treat-one-another-as-humans/.

3. See, for example, the online conversation with philmonomer, Thinking Christian blog, January 26, 2015, www.thinkingchristian.net/posts/2014/12/rhetorical-strategy-in-the-marriage-debate/#comment-110845.

4. "To Treat One Another As Humans: Part 2a," Thinking Christian blog, December 2, 2010, www.thinkingchristian.net/posts/2010/12/to-treat-one-another-as-humans-part-2a/.

to be treated—although it is an outstanding opportunity to apply the Golden Rule; it's right because we're all created in God's image.

As we go through this book, I will be talking about various ways Christians agree and disagree with LGBT beliefs, goals, and objectives. On these topics, we disagree much more than we agree. These are extremely important matters, so we'll spend a fair amount of time on them; we couldn't do them justice otherwise. But I wouldn't want that to overshadow the one most basic fact, going back to the very founding of the human race: we're all in this together. We're all humans made in God's image.

I will return to these same topics in chapter 5. For now, let's be sure always to keep our common humanity in mind, as we get back on the path toward understanding what marriage is, and why it is what it is.

A Case for Marriage from Two Perspectives

Marriage is between a man and a woman, or at least it always has been, until our current nanosecond eye-blink of history. Even polygamy is no exception: the man is married to the women, but the women aren't married to each other, except in rare cases. No major social group has ever considered same-sex unions to be marriage. The man–woman view of marriage has been consistent for virtually every human society throughout all time until *very* recently. The first law permitting same-sex marriage *anywhere* was enacted a scant decade and a half ago, in the Netherlands in the year 2000.[5]

Now, however, the US Supreme Court, along with the governments of many other Western countries, has chosen not only to disagree with the traditional definition but to close off all controversy. Marriage isn't necessarily between a man and a woman any longer. That debate is over.

And yet it continues. There are many among us who disagree

---

5. "Same-Sex Dutch Couples Gain Marriage and Adoption Rights," *The New York Times*, December 20, 2000, www.nytimes.com/2000/12/20/world/same-sex -dutch-couples-gain-marriage-and-adoption-rights.html.

strongly with the court's judgment. There may be little we can do about it politically for now, but we can still make our case biblically and morally. In fact, we have no choice but to keep making our case. Why? Because the whole world knows what we stand for. Our teens know what we stand for. To cease explaining our position would be like conceding that we were wrong all along. It would be the same as admitting that the rest of the world has been justified in thinking we never had any good reason to oppose same-sex marriage.

I wouldn't want my kids thinking that about me.

This isn't a lost cause that ought to be left in the rearview mirror. If anything, our case for marriage is more important now than before. We're not just arguing for a view of marriage; we're making a stand for the continuing, essential goodness of biblical principles, in spite of laws that contradict those principles.

So just as if the Supreme Court had never addressed the question, we need to think through what marriage really is and what it should be. Is the man–woman, natural view really what marriage is? That's an important question. Here's another one. Supposing that it is the right view, how would we know for sure?

My answer to the first question is, of course, yes, though I would expand the definition of marriage to include this: marriage is a *distinctive human good, the comprehensive union of a man and a woman*. I'll explain that in a moment.

The second question—*How would we know?*—has a dual answer. Those of us who believe in the Bible can find a clear enough answer there. Unsurprisingly, it's the same answer that people have given all over the world and throughout virtually all of human history, even without the Bible. That tells us there must be good reasons even apart from the Bible to see marriage that way. Scholars often call these reasons *natural-law arguments for marriage*. I'll just speak of them in terms of common human experience.

It's important to know something about both biblical and common-experience reasons for marriage to be for a man and a woman. I'll concentrate on the common-experience view of marriage for the rest of this chapter, and move on to biblical reasons in the next. I think it helps to start with common experience because it shows that marriage isn't just a matter of one's religious beliefs: there are many reasons for it, reasons that should have persuasive power among people who won't listen to what the Bible says. I'm beginning with the common-experience approach, too, because it allows room to explore some definitions and descriptions that will help us later on when it comes time to look at what the Bible says.

A Distinctive Human Good

In my definition above, I suggested that marriage is the comprehensive union of a man and a woman, and that it's also a distinctive human good. That latter part is important, because if marriage isn't distinctive it doesn't matter much what form it takes, and if it isn't good it isn't important enough to be worth fighting for. This definition for marriage isn't merely *important*, though; our common human experience tells us it's *true*.

Clearly, it's distinctive. Marriage is a form of friendship unlike any other. No other close friendship automatically implies sharing a name, a home, property, and funds. No other close friendship has the same social status. No other close friendship requires a license.

More important by far, though, no other close friendship matters so much to future generations. That's what makes marriage distinctively *good*. Any pair of people can provide each other good companionship. Any reasonably good relationship could be the basis for a good contractual partnership. Any two people can find sexual pleasure together. If that were all there was to marriage, there would be no reason to limit it to a man and a woman. It's distinctive mostly in this: marriage is the best place there is to raise the next generation.

Marriage's Most Distinctive Goodness

Marriage and children go together. There was a time (can anyone remember it anymore?) when, barring health issues, marriage *always* meant babies. Babies always meant marriage, too—marriage or scandal, that is. That was for good reason. Children need a stable, nurturing environment to grow up in, and there's none better than a home with their own mom and dad. That's what makes marriage a truly one-of-a-kind relationship.

It also explains why, unlike other forms of friendship, we have licenses and laws for marriage. Society is rightly interested in our future generations. Marriage laws have always served to unite dad with mom, relationally and financially, in the project of bringing up the next generation—and that's good for all of us.

There's plenty of research to support the fact that children grow up healthier in every way—physically, relationally, and emotionally—when they're with their mother and father (biological or adoptive). Sure, this rule has exceptions, especially when the parents' relationship is filled with conflict. When the parents' relationship is strong, though, children tend to grow up strong. Stable marriages are good for children.

They're even good for society at large. Consider this economic information from a paper delivered before the Council on Contemporary Families in 2002:

> Marriage offers important social and economic benefits. Children who grow up with married parents generally enjoy a higher standard of living than those living in single-parent households. Two parents are usually better than one not only because they can bring home two paychecks but also because they can share responsibilities for childcare. Marriage often leads to higher levels of paternal involvement than divorce, non-marriage, or cohabitation. Long-term commitments to provide love and support to one another are beneficial for adults, as well as children.[6]

Interestingly, this was written by a pair of researchers who wanted to caution public policy-makers against overstating the good that

---

6. Stephanie Coontz and Nancy Folbre, "Marriage, Poverty, and Public Policy: A Discussion Paper from the Council on Contemporary Families," paper prepared for the 5th annual Council on Contemporary Families conference, New York (April 26–28, 2002).

marriage can do. In other words, it's an example of the kind of statement researchers can make when they're being very careful not to oversell their point—yet it comes out as a powerful advertisement for marriage anyway.

Marriage is strongly associated with decreased poverty. Even researchers who are being terribly cautious support this point, too.[7]

I don't want to be insensitive toward single-parent families here. Millions of heroic single parents are raising families the hard way, and doing a great job of it. Millions of children are growing up without their own dad or mom at home, and they're demonstrating great strength in spite of it. Still, I've never met anyone who says they believe that growing up in a single-parent family is better than growing up in a home with two loving parents. And let's be completely honest: marriage is the best way anyone has ever found to keep a dad together with his kids and his kids' mom.

Apart from considerations relating to children, it's hard to think of any good reason to license and legislate marriage. It isn't because of the depth of friendship. It isn't even because of the sexual relationship (who wants the government involved in *that*?). It's because marriages mean families, including very young, very vulnerable family members who do a lot better when mom and dad are both there for them.

Which brings us back around to the reason marriage is specifically the comprehensive union of a man and a woman. Men and women are where kids come from, after all.

What About Children of Same-Sex Households?

You may have heard about research showing that same-sex couples' children turn out just as well as children raised with mom and dad. This topic is highly controversial, to say the least. Sorting out what to conclude from the research literature can be frustrating. I've found that when one person mentions a study supporting one view, someone else tosses back another study that supports the opposite

---

7. Emily Badger, "The Relationship Between Single Mothers and Poverty Is Not as Simple as It Seems," *Washington Post* Wonkblog (April 10, 2014).

view. Few people have the training to know which studies are done well and can therefore be trusted. So I want to offer three general perspectives to help you evaluate claims made by supporters of same-sex marriage.

First, no matter what you've heard, I can guarantee you there is no good research on the effects of same-sex parenting on children. None. *There couldn't be.* The entire phenomenon is too new. No study could be complete without following a group of children at least into adulthood, and then also following *their children* into adulthood. Child rearing isn't about the next *year* or even the next *decade*, it's about the next *generations*. No one will even begin to see the real results of this massive social experiment for another thirty years or more.

So if someone tells you there's good scientific research showing that children of same-sex couples do just as well as children raised by a mom and a dad, you can flatly answer that they're wrong. There could be no such research yet. The studies (such as they are) have barely begun, and the results we need most won't be in for a very long time to come. When the answer finally does come in, it might reveal one thing or it might show something else; either way, we just don't know yet, scientifically speaking.[8] Don't let the "experts" fool you on that.

Second, rarely if ever is there such a thing as unbiased social research, and in today's heavy-handed pro-LGBT environment, objective research into the effects of same-sex parenting is very unlikely indeed. We need to view every study—even those that seem to support our own views—through cautious eyes.

Third, among all the admittedly incomplete research that's been done, there is still some that is better than others. The best research, methodologically speaking (covering the largest, most scientifically-selected population samples), hints strongly that children of same-sex couples do less well than children raised by a mom and a dad.[9]

---

8. I believe I do know the answer on other grounds, but that's a different topic.
9. Three such studies: Mark Regnerus, "How Different Are the Adult Children of Parents Who Have Same-Sex Relationships? Findings from the New Family Structures Study," *Social Science Research* 41, no. 4 (2012); Mark Regnerus, "Parental Same-Sex Relationships, Family Instability, and Subsequent Life Outcomes for

These studies are not conclusive, because there haven't been enough children raised by same-sex couples to allow for solid statistical comparisons with children raised in other family structures. The results are strongly suggestive, however.

Not only that, but study after study supports the value of a loving home with both mom and dad in the picture.[10] It's only unfortunate that not every child has that home advantage.

Summary: What Marriage Is

We know what marriage has always been. Does that mean it must remain that way? Why can't marriage be expanded to include same-sex couples? I've already covered one reason: marriage is what it is, in the eyes of law and custom, because it's the best form of relationship for raising the next generation.

The fact is, if there were any good, solid reason to expand marriage to include same-sex couples, there would be little reason to stop there. The major reasons people give in favor of same-sex marriages are equally valid for same-sex or bisexual "throuples"—threesomes. As Fredrik DeBoer wrote in *Politico*, on the very day of the Supreme Court's approval of gay marriage,

> The marriage equality movement has been both the best and worst thing that could happen for legally sanctioned

---

Adult Children: Answering Critics of the New Family Structures Study With Additional Analyses," *Social Science Research* 41, no. 6 (2012); D. Paul Sullins, "Emotional Problems Among Children With Same-Sex Parents: Difference By Definition," *British Journal of Education, Society & Behavioural Science* 7, no. 2 (2015).

I mentioned a few paragraphs above that few of us are equipped to read and evaluate this kind of research. My master's degree in organizational psychology, a branch of social psychology, gives me some of the necessary background; and from my perspective, these studies were conducted well and reported responsibly. See also my further comments on the Sullins study under the Part 3 topic, "Gay and lesbian couples can be just as good parents as straight couples."

10. See the compendium of studies at Peter Spriggs, "'We know from the social sciences that children do best with a mom and a dad.'—TRUE," Family Research Council blog, October 17, 2014, www.frcblog.com/2014/10/we-know-social -science-children-do-best-mom-and-dad-true/.

polygamy. The best, because that movement has required a sustained and effective assault on "traditional marriage" arguments that reflected no particular point of view other than that marriage should stay the same because it's always been the same. In particular, the notion that procreation and child-rearing are the natural justification for marriage has been dealt a terminal injury.[11]

It was "the worst thing," he went on to say, mostly for political reasons, not for reasons of principle.

Justifications for gay marriage have also been used with equal logic to support incest, for example in Germany, where a government council has recommended the abolition of laws banning consensual relations between brothers and sisters.[12]

In other words, marriage definitions that go beyond one-man-with-one-woman go way too far. They can't help it. Either they cut off the number of partners at two just arbitrarily, for no principled reason, or else they end up encompassing virtually every imaginable "adult consenting relationship." If you follow the principles that seem to support gay marriage, you'll find that they also support forms of "marriage" that even most LGBT people would reject.

The only solid, reliable, principled definition of marriage is the one that requires it to be a man with a woman. That's what marriage always must be; otherwise, it isn't marriage. Men and women around the world until very, very recently have understood that much, even without benefit of God's revelation in the Bible. As we'll see in the next chapter, though, God's Word makes it even more abundantly clear.

---

11. Fredrik DeBoer, "It's Time to Legalize Polygamy: Why Group Marriage Is the Next Horizon of Social Liberalism," *Politico Magazine*, www.politico.com/maga zine/story/2015/06/gay-marriage-decision-polygamy-119469.html.

12. Damon Linker, "How Liberals Are Unwittingly Paving the Way for the Legalization of Adult Incest," *The Week*, September 30, 2014, theweek.com/articles/443410 /liberals-are-unwittingly-paving-way-legalization-adult-incest.

CHAPTER FOUR

Marriage and Morality in the Bible

We've seen that natural marriage is a distinctive human good, and that virtually everyone throughout all time has been able to see—even without referring to the Scriptures— that it is for a man and a woman.

For those of us who acknowledge the Bible as God's Word, though, the case for natural marriage is far stronger yet. Marriage was in God's plan from the beginning. It's strongly implied in the first chapter of Genesis (Gen. 1:27–28), and its proper form is plainly stated just one chapter later, in Genesis 2:24: "Therefore a man shall leave his father and his mother and hold fast to his wife, and they shall become one flesh." Jesus reaffirmed that message in the strongest possible terms:

> And Pharisees came up to him and tested him by asking, "Is it lawful to divorce one's wife for any cause?" He answered, "Have you not read that he who created them from the beginning made them male and female, and said, 'Therefore a man shall leave his father and his mother and hold fast to his wife, and the two shall become one flesh'? So they are no longer two but one flesh. What therefore God has joined

together, let not man separate." They said to him, "Why then did Moses command one to give a certificate of divorce and to send her away?" He said to them, "Because of your hardness of heart Moses allowed you to divorce your wives, but from the beginning it was not so. And I say to you: whoever divorces his wife, except for sexual immorality, and marries another, commits adultery." (Matt. 19:3–9)

Marriage was a symbol of God's relationship with his people in the Old Testament, especially in the first three chapters of the book of Hosea, where God told the prophet to take Gomer as his wife, specifically to illustrate Israel's relationship with God. It's even more so in the New Testament. For example, Ephesians 5:22–32:

> Wives, submit to your own husbands, as to the Lord. For the husband is the head of the wife even as Christ is the head of the church, his body, and is himself its Savior. Now as the church submits to Christ, so also wives should submit in everything to their husbands.
>
> Husbands, love your wives, as Christ loved the church and gave himself up for her, that he might sanctify her, having cleansed her by the washing of water with the word, so that he might present the church to himself in splendor, without spot or wrinkle or any such thing, that she might be holy and without blemish. In the same way husbands should love their wives as their own bodies. He who loves his wife loves himself. For no one ever hated his own flesh, but nourishes and cherishes it, just as Christ does the church, because we are members of his body. "Therefore a man shall leave his father and mother and hold fast to his wife, and the two shall become one flesh." This mystery is profound, and I am saying that it refers to Christ and the church.

The marriage theme pervades the Bible to the very end:

Then I heard what seemed to be the voice of a great mul-
titude, like the roar of many waters and like the sound of
mighty peals of thunder, crying out,
> "Hallelujah!
> For the Lord our God
>   the Almighty reigns.
> Let us rejoice and exult
>   and give him the glory,
> for the marriage of the Lamb has come,
>   and his Bride has made herself ready;
> it was granted her to clothe herself
>   with fine linen, bright and pure"—

for the fine linen is the righteous deeds of the saints.
And the angel said to me, "Write this: Blessed are those
who are invited to the marriage supper of the Lamb." And he
said to me, "These are the true words of God." . . .
And I saw the holy city, new Jerusalem, coming down out
of heaven from God, prepared as a bride adorned for her
husband. . . .
The Spirit and the Bride say, "Come."
>   (Rev. 19:6–9; 21:2; 22:17)

It's in the Bible's first chapters, it's in its last chapters, it's affirmed
strongly by Jesus, and there's absolutely no hint of any other model
for it. Marriage—natural marriage between a man and a woman—is
central to God's plan for humans.

It Was Never "Just You and Me, Babe"

Do you recall our discussion on "just you and me, babe" in
chapter 2? Marriage took a strange and disastrous turn when that
inward-looking attitude infiltrated culture in the 1960s.

"Just you and me, babe" marriage has hurt generations of children.
It started out as a deep crack in heterosexual marriage culture. The
fault lines have spread since then. Same-sex marriage is overwhelmingly about "just you and me, babe" relationships. Whatever form they

take—whether they involve a same-sex couple or a man and a woman—"just you and me, babe" relationships violate one of Scripture's most consistent principles: when God gives a blessing, it isn't just so the person can enjoy it for himself. It's so he can pass it along.

No good thing is primarily inward-looking. We see this pattern throughout the Bible, from God's promise to Abraham in Genesis 12:3 ("in you all the families of the earth shall be blessed") to the second Great Commandment in Matthew 22:39 ("love your neighbor as yourself"), to the great love chapter, 1 Corinthians 13 ("but the greatest of these is love"). God's way has always been other-oriented, never inward-focused. He sacrificed himself for us as an expression of his overflowing, other-centered love (see Rom. 5:8).

Surely the same principle applies to couples: when God gives a couple a blessing, it's so they can pass it along. Marital love was meant to grow and to overflow, outward from the couple, into the incredibly other-oriented task of raising children.

I'm convinced that for my wife and me, parenting has been one of God's chief means of growing us up into Christlike selflessness (as far as we have grown in it, that is). My friend Chuck said once, "I used to have the Spirit-filled life all figured out. Then I had children." One of his children was born with kidney disease; he has had more than one transplant, along with many other operations. Through that decades-long trial, Chuck has become one of the wisest and most Christ-centered mentors and teachers I know.

Marriage isn't for "just you and me, babe." It's a God-ordained institution for the growth and overflow of love, nurturance, and care—for the sake of the couple, yes, but even more for the sake of future generations. That alone is a sufficient biblical answer to the most common arguments for same-sex marriage.

There's more, though. We have not yet broached the question of sexual morality.

Sexual Morality in the Bible

We've been talking about marriage in particular. What does the Bible say about sexual activity in general? This answer is even clearer;

in fact, hardly anything is plainer in Scripture than its teachings on sexual morality. Sexual relationships are for married persons, and no one else. Do we even need to look at the passages in detail? The list is long. In the New Testament alone, we have Matthew 5:32; 15:19; Mark 7:21; Acts 15:20, 29; 21:25; Romans 13:13; 1 Corinthians 5:1, 11; 6:13, 18; 7:2; 10:8; 2 Corinthians 12:21; Galatians 5:19; Ephesians 5:3; Colossians 3:5; 1 Thessalonians 4:3; Jude 7; and Revelation 2:14, 20; 9:21; 14:8; 17:2, 4; 18:3, 9.

The Greek word used in all these locations except one (Rom. 13:3) is *porneia*, or some variation on the same root word. It means "fornication . . . illicit sex in general"[1] or "to engage in sexual immorality of any kind, often with the implication of prostitution—'to engage in illicit sex, to commit fornication, sexual immorality, fornication, prostitution.'"[2]

Does Sexual Morality Really Matter That Much?

Why is sex such a big deal in the Bible? There are many reasons; but remember, it isn't just a big deal there. It's a big deal—in quite a different way—everywhere you look, from the Internet to advertisements to on-campus relationships. The world overplays it and cheapens it. God has a better plan in mind. Once I heard a girl, about fourteen years old, say in a youth group meeting, "I don't get what's the big deal about a kiss on a first date." I shot back, "Not a big deal!? Every kiss I've ever shared with my wife has been a big deal! I love that it's a big deal! Why would anyone want it to be anything less than a big deal?"

Sex matters, and it should. It matters both for good and for bad. It matters because of its incredible motivational power (for good or for bad). It matters because it leads to childbirth. It matters because it has

---

1. Joseph Henry Thayer, *Thayer's Greek-English Lexicon of the New Testament*, 1889 edition, reprinted by Hendrickson Publishers, Rei Sub edition (August 1, 1995). Accessed via Accordance software for Macintosh, n.p.

2. J. P. Louw and E. A. Nida, *Vol. 1: Greek-English Lexicon of the New Testament: Based on Semantic Domains*, electronic ed. of the 2nd ed. (New York: United Bible Societies, 1996), 770.

such potential (for good) to be other-oriented, giving, overflowing from the couple into future generations not yet born, or else (for bad) to be one of the most self-centered, deeply damaging acts there could be. I say that very soberly. I had a first cousin who died at the hands of a man who made sex a matter of his own cruel pleasure.

For good or bad, sex is life-changing. It has a huge influence on our decisions and our direction. It matters. It matters whether or not we live out our sexual desires and relationships in a good way; and that's what sexual morality is about, isn't it?

Sex was meant for a loving couple, committed to one another in covenant relationship, expressing that relationship in the deepest possible way, and yet with a love not confined to themselves but open to its overflowing into even more love, more Christlike giving, more self-sacrifice.

The Bible's Word on Homosexual Practices

If sex outside of marriage is wrong (which it is), and if marriage is for a man and a woman (which it is), then it follows that homosexual sex is wrong. Need I say more? Yet that's not all we have to go on, because the Bible makes its views on same-sex intimacy doubly clear:

> You shall not lie with a male as with a woman; it is an abomination. (Lev. 18:22)

> If a man lies with a male as with a woman, both of them have committed an abomination; they shall surely be put to death; their blood is upon them. (Lev. 20:13)

> Or do you not know that the unrighteous will not inherit the kingdom of God? Do not be deceived: neither the sexually immoral, nor idolaters, nor adulterers, nor men who practice homosexuality, nor thieves, nor the greedy, nor drunkards, nor revilers, nor swindlers will inherit the kingdom of God. (1 Cor. 6:9–10)

> Understanding this, that the law is not laid down for the just but for the lawless and disobedient, for the ungodly and sinners, for the unholy and profane, for those who strike their fathers

and mothers, for murderers, the sexually immoral, men who practice homosexuality, enslavers, liars, perjurers, and whatever else is contrary to sound doctrine. (1 Tim. 1:9–10)

And especially,

For this reason God gave them up to dishonorable passions. For their women exchanged natural relations for those that are contrary to nature; and the men likewise gave up natural relations with women and were consumed with passion for one another, men committing shameless acts with men and receiving in themselves the due penalty for their error. . . .

Though they know God's righteous decree that those who practice such things deserve to die, they not only do them but give approval to those who practice them. (Rom. 1:26–27, 32)

Some pro-LGBT writers say these passages only apply to ritual sex as practiced in pagan temple worship or to a certain sort of male–male relationship that simply doesn't exist anymore. Therefore, they say, these prohibitions do not apply to committed, monogamous same-sex relationships (gay marriage, in other words). They often go so far as to say the Bible actually supports gay marriage.

I will go into more detail on these views in part 3, in the topic titled "The New Testament isn't talking about committed, monogamous same-sex marriage." The short answer is simple enough for now, though: no biblical interpreter, no historian, no original-language linguist—no one, in other words—ever gave that idea a moment's thought or the slightest credence until around the time of the sexual revolution in the 1960s. If God had meant us to see that message in his Word, we ought to have discovered it a long time ago. Those who seem to have found it there now have a bias that leads them to want (or even need) to find it there. I think they've read it into the text, rather than reading it from the text as responsible Bible students do.

Summary

It should be clear enough now: both the Bible and common human experience support the reality that marriage is for a man and a woman, and sexual practice is for married couples.

There's much more to be said about these topics. Since it's such an overwhelmingly important issue in our day—for the moral debate still rages on, even if the legal one has been decided—I urge you to read more, especially the books and articles I've included in the resource guide at the end of this book.

Part Two

NAVIGATING THE ROCKY RELATIONSHIPS

CHAPTER FIVE
Relating in Truth, Love, and Strength

So far we've looked at some of the origins of gay-rights advocacy, and we've clarified a biblical way of looking at the issues. Now it's time to turn to the question, "How do we equip our children—not to mention ourselves—for a world where gay rights are 'right' and Christian beliefs are considered wrong?" Our goal in everything must be to live and relate to others in love and in truth. We may be accused of intentionally harming LGBT people. We should never let that accusation be true. At the same time we dare not forget that failing to speak the truth can be harmful, too.

I'm talking to parents here, though, and I'm well aware of the way parental instincts can kick in. It's a crazy world out there. It's regressed to the point where homosexuality is no longer just tolerated, it's celebrated, while Christianity is treated with contempt. In a world like that, is it wise to let our children be in relationship with LGBT people?

I would suggest that's the wrong question. If they're in a class, part of a music group, or on a sports team with a gay or lesbian person, they *are* in a relationship with them—whether you're comfortable with it or not. For most teens, the question isn't *whether* they have that relationship; it's *what kind* of relationship they have.

Our World Has Shifted

I remember one evening in college, back in the mid-1970s, when my friends and I were praying for persecuted Christians in the Soviet Union. Someone said, "Do you suppose the day could ever come when Christianity would be persecuted here in America?" We agreed it was theoretically possible, but impossible to imagine. It isn't impossible anymore. Obviously, and tragically, Christians in parts of Africa, Asia, and the Middle East are suffering far more for their faith than we are. By the standard Jesus spoke of in the Beatitudes, however ("when others revile you and persecute you and utter all kinds of evil against you falsely on my account"—Matt. 5:11–12), persecution is going on here, too. It used to be that church was for people who wanted to be good (or look good, at least). Now believers are regarded as hateful, shameful, and evil. The early church might have experienced something like this,[1] but we never have, until very recently. There's always been spiritual conflict. For us, now, it's come out into the open. It's a dizzyingly unfamiliar reality.

But there's something not quite accurate in what I just wrote. For you and me it's unfamiliar. For our teens, it's the only world they've ever known. Yet we are the ones who must train and equip them for it.

Spiritual Battle God's Way

When it comes to spiritual battle, most Christians think first of Ephesians 6:11–18, with its comprehensive list of battle armor: truth, righteousness, the readiness of the gospel of peace, faith, salvation, the Word of God, and prayer.

The Bible has much more to say about spiritual battle than that, however. The following passage in 2 Corinthians 10:3–5 is classic, especially for clashes over what's really true:

---

1. More often than not, when the early church fathers wrote in defense of the faith, the charge they were answering was that there was something evil about Christianity. See William Edgar and K. Scott Oliphint, eds., *Christian Apologetics Past and Present (Volume 1, to 1500): A Primary Source Reader* (Wheaton, IL: Crossway, 2009).

For though we walk in the flesh, we are not waging war according to the flesh. For the weapons of our warfare are not of the flesh but have divine power to destroy strongholds. We destroy arguments and every lofty opinion raised against the knowledge of God, and take every thought captive to obey Christ.

In 2 Corinthians 6:7, Paul speaks of "truthful speech, and the power of God," in connection with "weapons of righteousness for the right hand and for the left." *Nave's Topical Bible* explains that the right and left hand here refer to "attack and defend."[2]

Paul urges Timothy, in 1 Timothy 1:18–19, to "wage the good warfare, holding faith and a good conscience."

Three times we're taught that God opposes the proud (there's conflict implied in that, isn't there?) but gives grace to the humble (Prov. 3:34; James 4:6; 1 Peter 5:5). If we want to stand a chance in any battle, we'd better not invite God's opposition by carrying pride into the fight with us.

Conflict God's Way

All this talk of warfare and weapons—doesn't it sound terribly nasty and violent? It's a figure of speech, obviously, and yet there is real conflict going on, too. Is it bad to be in conflict? Not if we engage in it God's way. The Christian call to action is a call to good things, including righteousness, for example: not *self-righteousness*, which is ugly, but living in right and just relationships, beginning with our relationship with God.

It's also a call to *faith, truth, love, humility,* and *seeking the power of God.* As parents, we need to know and practice these things, so our teens can see them in action. At the right time and in the right way (more in chapter 6) we need to teach them these principles, too. Those five topics are worth spending more time on. I'll begin with *faith.*

---

2. Orville J. Nave, *Nave's Topical Bible* (Grand Rapids: Zondervan, 1999).

Faith

Faith has come under fire lately from prominent atheists who want us to think it means "belief without evidence." Even some Christians think that's what faith is. It isn't.[3] Dr. Timothy McGrew gave a much more accurate definition during a 2014 radio debate with atheist Peter Boghossian.[4] McGrew explained that faith is "trusting, holding to, acting on what one has reason to think is true, even in the face of difficulties," or, "to engage in a course of action whose outcome you care about, when the outcome is outside your control." In other words, while faith goes beyond what we can see or control, it's always grounded in something we have reason to think is true. For the topic under discussion here, that "something" is the biblical and common-experience knowledge we have about marriage and morality—the sorts of things we looked at in chapters 3 and 4. Faith begins with that kind of knowledge. From there it moves on to trusting, holding on to, or acting on that knowledge—even if it's difficult, and even when you can't control the outcome.

Faith Means Taking Risks

Someone once said, "Faith is spelled R-I-S-K." There may be some acts of faith that involve little risk, but standing strong on the issue of homosexuality is not one of them. Brendan Eich lost his job as CEO of the Mozilla Corporation because of his donation supporting Proposition 8 in California (which made same-sex marriage illegal in 2008). Others have been fined and sentenced to "sensitivity training" for standing firm for natural marriage.

Most teenagers' jobs won't be put at risk because of their convictions, but their academic careers could be, especially when they get

---

3. For more on this, see Tom Gilson, *Peter Boghossian, Atheist Tactician: A Preliminary Response to* A Manual for Creating Atheists, 2013, Kindle.

4. Audio (mp3 file) at Peter Boghossian, Timothy McGrew, and Justin Brierley, "Unbelievable (With Justin Brierley) Radio Programme, McGrew-Boghossian Debate," 2014. Text-based summary (live blog) at Tom Gilson "McGrew -Boghossian Debate Live Blog," 2014: www.thinkingchristian.net/posts/2014/05 /mcgrew-boghossian-debate-live-blog/.

to college. Their friendships may be deeply strained—and there's nothing so important to most teens as their friendships! Outspoken Christian youth face a huge risk of being shamed and ridiculed. It's never easy to go against the crowd.

We can't control those outcomes. We can predict some of them fairly well, though, and that's where faith comes in. Do we believe what God says about marriage and morality? That's a good start. Do we also believe he'll take care of us if we risk ourselves for that belief? That's the kind of faith we need to pass along. Our teens won't catch it from us if we don't have it ourselves.

Jesus's Brand of Risk

Jesus told his disciples, "I am sending you out as sheep in the midst of wolves" (Matt. 10:16). Pause a moment and think about what that means. "There are wild animals out there. They roam in packs. They have big teeth. You look tasty to them. And now I'm sending you out among them, without any defense of your own against them." Sure, it's metaphorical, but still you get the picture: staying safe is not what Jesus had in mind for us. Actually his instructions sound almost stupid: why go out where we're likely to get torn in pieces? But it isn't foolish at all. It's living in faith—faith in the one who also told his disciples,

> The thief comes only to steal and kill and destroy. I came that they may have life and have it abundantly. I am the good shepherd. The good shepherd lays down his life for the sheep. He who is a hired hand and not a shepherd, who does not own the sheep, sees the wolf coming and leaves the sheep and flees, and the wolf snatches them and scatters them. He flees because he is a hired hand and cares nothing for the sheep. I am the good shepherd. (John 10:10–14)

Yes, there are wolves out there, but there's also a shepherd watching out for the sheep—not just casually, like a hireling, but with a true shepherd's love. He lays down his life for his sheep. The sheep are okay—in fact, under this Shepherd there is abundant life. In John

16:33 he said, "In the world you will have tribulation. But take heart; I have overcome the world."

The wolves don't win in the end.

What Does It Take to Live in Faith?

God's Word tells us we can count on him overcoming through us. When the pressure is on, we need confidence in the truth of God and his Word to be able to keep holding on. That's what faith is about: being confident God's Word is true no matter how much our circumstances seem stacked up against it.

The LGBT issue is nothing but a faith and truth challenge, the biggest one the Western church has faced in generations. On a societal level, nothing else in recent memory has involved so much confusion, so much conflict, so much potential loss—so much difficulty and risk, in other words.

Jesus Christ is calling us to believe he'll keep us safe and strong in his care. He's calling us to have faith.

Truth

Faith goes with truth, and truth with faith. It does no good to believe in what's false, or to be weak and untrusting toward what's true.

Yet it's so easy to back down from what we know to be true! Somehow we've gotten the idea that we're supposed to keep quiet. There are voices out there telling us not to speak the truth on marriage and morality. It's going to "sound intolerant," they say, or it might "harm people." But Jesus came "full of grace *and* truth" (John 1:14, emphasis added; see also John 1:17). Ephesians 4:15 tells us to speak the truth in love. In Christ there is no contradiction between truth, grace, and love.

The truth has power. (I often wonder if that's why it's unwelcome in so many places.) The Word of God is "the sword of the Spirit" of Ephesians 6:17, "sharper than any two-edged sword" for discerning the inner person (Heb. 4:12). The spiritual battle described in 2 Corinthians 10:3–5 is a battle for truth, and indeed its chief weapon is truth. Craig Keener put it this way in his commentary on that passage: "Greek sages sometimes described their battle against false ideas as a war, in terms similar to those Paul uses here. Like those sages, Paul claims to be doing battle with false ideas."[5]

Jesus spoke truth without flinching. He came carrying grace to rescue us from our sins, yet he was never hesitant to name sin what it truly was. He told the woman caught in adultery, "Neither do I condemn you"; but he also said, "Go, and from now on sin no more" (John 8:11).

We can follow his example: neither condemning others nor shrinking back from speaking God's truth. This means we have to know the truth, meaning of course all of God's Word, but especially—since this is where we're being tested so much these days—what God says about relationships, moral purity, and marriage. Having a good grasp on the truth, we can stand by it as Jesus did.

You might wonder what this looks like in practice. The answer encompasses this entire book, which from first to last is about understanding and practicing the truth in an often-hostile culture.

Love

If there's anything more challenging than standing for what's true, it's standing for it in love: earnestly, consistently seeking what's best for the other person.

The task has been complicated in our culture by the rise of a new so-called virtue: tolerance. Watch out: it's a sham. As I will explain further in part 3 ("Why are you so intolerant?"), tolerance is a weak, insidious counterfeit for love. For me to be "tolerant" means I've decided not to let you and your beliefs bother me. I could do that by just ignoring you. You could have your space in the world, you could play your music, you could wear your fashions and speak your language, you could do what you please in the privacy of your bedroom, and I could tolerate it all just by choosing not to pay any attention to you.

---

5. Craig S. Keener, *The IVP Bible Background Commentary: New Testament,* Accordance electronic ed. (Downers Grove, IL: InterVarsity Press, 1993), 508.

Some LGBT people say all they want is to be left alone to live their lives their way. I doubt it. The opposite of love isn't hate, but apathy; and apathy lives right next door to what passes for tolerance these days. True biblical love, in contrast, involves connection, respect, and seeking the best. You can't love the one you avoid.

Love in Action

As the parent, you may or may not have any real relationships with out-of-the-closet LGBT individuals. If your child is in a Christian school or home school, he or she may not either. But if your teen is in public school or a secular university, it's almost certain that he or she does. Whatever your connection with LGBT people might be, true Christian love says not to avoid them. First Corinthians 5:9–10 says, "I wrote to you in my letter not to associate with sexually immoral people—not at all meaning the sexually immoral of this world, or the greedy and swindlers, or idolaters, since then you would need to go out of the world." I'll return to that passage in chapter 7.

Love treats the other person as you would want to be treated: first of all as a human being who is worthy of God's love the same as you, me, or our children.

Listening

There is no better way to connect than by listening and hearing others' stories. I've gained more understanding and appreciation for gay friends that way than any other. When a man tells me, "I've tried, but I just cannot imagine being attracted to a woman," I could condemn him or I could appreciate his vulnerability and open up to him about my own struggles. For me, that was exactly the kind of thing that opened the door to my most significant friendship with a gay man. Sure, we disagree on the morality of homosexual practice. We both know that. He knows, too (I've asked him), that I love him, and I sense the same from him.

God loves sinners. That means me. It means LGBT people, too.

I know of no better Christian example for this attitude than

Andrew Marin, as he tells of it in *Love Is an Orientation*.[6] It was through listening to what he had learned that I myself learned that LGBT individuals often dislike being labeled or described as *homosexual*. Does it matter whether we respect others' preferences on matters like that? If we have to shade the truth to do so, then, yes, it matters. "LGBT" is accurate, though, and choosing to identify others by terminology they prefer is one way to respect them as fellow human beings.[7]

If it's hard for you to imagine developing a friendship with a gay man, a lesbian, or a transgender person, consider this. I wrote in chapter 2 that you've been overhauled. Your children have been overhauled. That overhauling was accomplished by activists, a minority of LGBT people. I believe the majority of LGBT persons today have been overhauled just as much as you and I have, if not more so. They've been subjected to false images and propaganda concerning Christianity, too. That barrage of rhetoric has to have had an effect on their beliefs about their sexuality and about Christianity, too. They've been fed a lot of misinformation, so if they have false beliefs about Christian faith, it's easy to see where that came from.

It's almost certain that you and I have false beliefs about life as an LGBT person, too. The category of *transgender*, for example, encompasses so many different sets of feelings and beliefs, no one could possibly know what it means in the life of someone who identifies that way without actually hearing them explain it. Does it matter if we understand? Yes—because it's an act of love. Listening doesn't imply agreement. It does communicate caring.

(Of course there are some LGBT people who don't want us anywhere near them because of our beliefs, and we need to respect that. We can regret it for their sakes, but we need to respect it.)

---

6. Andrew Marin, *Love Is an Orientation: Elevating the Conversation with the Gay Community* (Downers Grove, IL: IVP Books, 2009).

7. Some observers consider "LGBT" to be capitulating to gays and lesbians in equating their sexuality with their identity. Whether that criticism has merit is a question that's beyond the scope of this book, and I do not think it would be helpful either to parents or to teens to make an issue of it here.

Touch

Next to listening, it seems the next most important way to connect is a very simple one: a friendly touch or casual shoulder hug. That may sound like strange advice. Some people shrink back as if there were something wrong with touching a gay man or a lesbian. There isn't. That is stereotypical thinking. By pushing past those false beliefs, we're showing we're not afraid and that we recognize the person's real humanity.

Think of it this way. The word *homophobia* is misused and inaccurate in nearly every case, but not always. To shrink away from a friendly hug just might indicate a fear of "catching something." I'm not talking about HIV/AIDS—most of us know there's no reason to be afraid of that in casual contact. I'm talking about something more like the old playground idea of "cooties." Cooties are creatures of a confused imagination—though with real effects because they create separation, animosity, and distrust. To fear or avoid contact with an LGBT person really is phobic; it's one of the few cases where the term *homophobia* fits.

Humility

What if you think there really is something unworthy about LGBT people? It's time to remember Romans 5:6–8: "For while we were still weak, at the right time Christ died for the ungodly. For one will scarcely die for a righteous person—though perhaps for a good person one would dare even to die—but God shows his love for us in that while we were still sinners, Christ died for us." That includes you and me, and no matter how much we love them, it includes our children. Remember, too, that Paul spoke the truth about himself when he described himself as the worst of sinners (see 1 Tim. 1:15). I, too, am the worst of all sinners. I don't know anyone who isn't. So if you think the LGBT person you're with is unworthy of you, remember how unworthy you are before God, yet he loved you enough to die for you—and for the LGBT person, too.

The Power of God

"Finally, be strong in the Lord and in the strength of his might" (Eph. 6:10). That's how Paul opens up his classic passage on spiritual warfare, already mentioned above. "We do not wrestle against flesh and blood," he goes on to teach, "but against the rulers, against the authorities, against the cosmic powers over this present darkness, against the spiritual forces of evil in the heavenly places" (v. 12).

In all the controversy, all the media discussions, all the constant maneuverings going on around the gay-rights controversy, we must never forget that there's more going on than meets the eye. This battle for the hearts and minds of our children is too intense for us to fight on our own.

The challenges are daunting. Gay marriage won in the Supreme Court. Those who oppose it are becoming a minority, and we're facing an overwhelming pro-LGBT onslaught orchestrated by the media, supported by educators, and endorsed by governments. Or so it seems; but again, there's more going on than meets the eye. The God who created the universe and who came and conquered sin and death is the same God in whose kingdom we serve. He is victor, and he will reign victoriously.

No matter how things look, we are not losers. We aren't even underdogs. Both you and your teen can stand strong—but only if you stand in the might of the Lord, the strength that comes out of a close, vital, prayerful relationship with God.

As the parent, you're in a prime position to lead, coach, teach, guide, and correct your child. Make the most of it. Be strong in faith, in truth, in love, and in prayer and the Holy Spirit.

CHAPTER SIX

Talking with Your Teen About Tough Questions: Basic Principles

It's time to get more practical now. I know what many parents must be thinking by this point: *This is all well and good, but do you have any clue how hard it's going to be to talk with my teen about any of this?*

It's awkward, no doubt, but there are ways to break through that discomfort. I'm so grateful that my son and daughter, now in college and beyond, have felt the freedom to remain open with us as parents. We haven't been perfect parents—far from it—but we've found ways to keep lines of communication open with them. I'm sure there's a lot they keep to themselves and to their close friends, which is normal and natural. Yet I believe we know them and they generally feel safe with us.

In this chapter I share five principles I've learned through my own experience and the experience of others for talking with your teen about tough subjects—general principles that you can apply to much more than LGBT issues.

1. Ask Good Questions

Every parent wants their teen to be open with them. One of the best ways to help them open up is by asking good questions. (Jesus was a master at asking questions!) Here are some example questions for you to consider asking your teen.

- Do you have any gay, lesbian, bisexual, or transgender friends? What's it like for you when they talk about their relationships or their feelings?
- What do you think about gay marriage being allowed now?
- Do your friends think of Christians as being anti-gay? What do you sense they're saying about your own views? Do they know what you think about it?
- Do *you* know what you think about the whole issue?
- Which gay-rights issues make the most sense to you? Which ones don't make sense to you?
- What questions have come up in school about gay rights? Have you discussed LGBT issues in any of your classes?
- Does it make you uncomfortable that our church preaches and teaches against homosexuality? What would your friends say if they heard that message?
- Have you ever wished that Christians could just drop this whole issue completely?
- What would you say most of your friends think about gay rights and other LGBT concerns?
- Could you imagine your student body electing a transgender person as prom queen?

Obviously some of these fall into the category of dangerous questions—dangerous for your teen, that is. He or she may wonder, *Should I answer what I think, or what my parents want to hear?* If they're not sure it's safe to say what they think, they're going to go with what they think you want to hear, not with what's really on their mind. That leads directly to my next point.

2. Be a Safe Listener

If we want our teens to share openly with us, we need to be safe people for them to share with. But what does it mean to be a *safe* listener when you're the parent, and when the questions are this potentially risky?

Obviously it involves caring enough to take the time to listen. That's basic. Yet you're the parent, and your kids know what that means: you're in charge. You're not their buddy. You hold a lot of power in their lives, so there's a sense in which you could be unavoidably dangerous.

So how can a parent make it safe for teens to open up?

Love Them No Matter What

The most basic principle, and the most crucial answer, is that your teen must know that you truly love him and seek his best. He has to know you love him *unconditionally, no matter what,* and that *nothing* he could say or do would alter your love toward him or make you accept him any less.

I've checked in with my own children about this more than once. I'm a Christian apologist, which means it's my vocational focus to explain and defend the truth of Christianity. That has put pressure on my kids to believe what I believe, as a vocational belief-defender-persuader.

I don't want them to believe because of that pressure, though. I want them to own their faith for themselves. So I've asked them, "If you ever had doubts about the truth of Christianity, would you feel the freedom to say so? Would you feel the freedom to say you are having trouble believing?" Thankfully, so far they've said yes. It's vitally important that they have freedom to share what's on their hearts. I want them always to know that. I want them to know, too, that no matter what kinds of questions they might have, I will always love and support them.

Make It Even Safer

Unconditional love gets you a good way toward being a safe listener with your teens. For the really tough issues, though, you'll need to go even further.

Think how threatening it might be for a teen to admit to her parent that she has questions about homosexuality, has bisexual friends, or just wishes you would keep quiet about this whole issue so she wouldn't get picked on. How could you make it feel safe for her to speak honestly?

One way would be to start with questions like the ones I suggested above. Keep your ears open for a what-mom-or-dad-wants-to-hear sort of answer. If she answers that way, add a follow-up question: "I'm glad to hear you say that, but I'm also a little surprised. I'd think that most of your friends would say something different. So if you're feeling something different, just know that it wouldn't surprise me, it wouldn't upset me, and I'd sure like to listen to what you have to say about it."

You need to be honest about this. Remember the old saying, "Always be sincere, but if you can't be sincere, at least fake it"? You can forget about that one! It won't work with teens. They can tell. When you tell them it wouldn't surprise or upset you, and that you really would like to listen, they'll know if you're telling the truth or not. So resolve to listen, and listen *well*, no matter what.

Respond, Don't React

You're asking your teen to be honest with you. That means they might say just about anything. Whatever your teen may say, be mentally prepared to respond, not react. That's easier said than done, especially if your teen comes out with something really disturbing or something that's really wrong in your eyes. So be prepared for *anything* your kids might say; and whatever comes out of their mouth, *respond*, don't *react*.

Even if you're caught totally off guard, you could still say something like, "Wow. I wasn't expecting you to say that. Let me think about it a bit, and let's talk about it some more tomorrow. I'm glad you felt free to share that with me." Then be sure to have that conversation the next day. Acknowledge that these are some of the hardest issues there are—especially at their age, when they're getting tugged and pulled in every direction. Assure them it's okay to bring that tugging and pulling out into the open. Let them know you're there to explore it with them—whatever "it" might be.[1]

Accept the Necessary Risk

If I could force my kids into doing right and being right all the time, I'd do it in an instant! That's not how parenting works, though, is it? Teens' primary task is to grow into the maturity of fully independent adulthood. They have to develop their own convictions. There comes a time when we have to give them freedom to do that— even at the risk that they'll get some things wrong. After all, God does the same for his children.

We can still coach our teens, though, and guide them as they think things through. With prayer, the work of the Holy Spirit, and judicious advice on our part, there's a great chance they'll land in a good place.

In fact, for most young people there's a better chance they'll come out spiritually strong, emotionally mature, and relationally healthy through a parent-guided questioning process than if we shut them down, react, or dismiss their questions altogether. I have a story about that, actually, and it forms the basis of my third principle for connecting with teens.

3. Don't Brush Off Questions

My wife and I sat appalled. A friend of ours was telling the story of her background. We had known her for years, or thought we had. She and her family were deeply involved in our church. That evening, though, we found out that her spiritual journey had not been what we'd been led to believe. She had been faking it. Recently—finally!— she had made a genuine, life-changing turn to the Lord.

That evening she told us the rest of the story. A lot had gone wrong, and it all began in her teenage years when the leaders in her church

---

1. Bear in mind, please, that this is about conversations with teens. The younger the child, the more your response might be along the lines of teaching, correction, and discipline.

told her she shouldn't ask hard questions. Her recent return to Christ had begun when she discovered authors like Tim Keller, who took seriously her kinds of questions and gave believable biblical answers.

I can't tell you how often I've heard people say, "They told me at my church not to ask questions, but just to believe." In my experience, almost every one of those people turned to disbelief. Some of them came back to faith, but not all.

Take Questions Seriously

In chapter 1 I mentioned research showing that teens who have the freedom to express and explore their doubts tend to stay in the faith more than teens who are stifled, told they must believe, or commanded not to ask hard questions. Sometimes, though, what shuts them down isn't so much a command to keep quiet as it is an atmosphere in which they just know, *We don't ask those kinds of questions here. We don't talk about those things.* Whether at home or at church, that's not good for kids. They're asking those kinds of questions somewhere. Wouldn't you rather one of those places be at home, with you?

Young people need to explore their doubts freely. Our role in that exploration is to take their questions seriously. (This isn't only about homosexuality; it's about everything related to life and faith.) Think of it this way: if we send them signals that their questions are too dangerous to ask, what are they going to think? *My parents are afraid—afraid someone else might be right and they might be wrong. If they weren't so afraid they wouldn't run from it. Or maybe they're just ignorant, closed-minded, behind the times. I'm going to go find someone else who will take my questions seriously.* And who knows who that someone might be, or what that someone might tell them?

Avoid the Biblical Brush-Off

One way not to take questions seriously is by answering, "It's in the Bible, so believe it." The fact is, you can't command belief that way. It doesn't work in religion, any more than it does anywhere else.

Suppose your boss tells you one morning, "We bought you an iPad, I hope you find it helpful in your work."

You answer, "Great! When is it coming?"

He responds, "It's right there on your desk."

"That's funny—I don't see it here."

"Oh, but there it is, right next to your coffee cup."

"Uhh, I'm having trouble believing that: if it were there, I think I'd see it. My desk isn't *that* messy."

"Now, hold on. I'm your boss, and I'm telling you to believe me. It doesn't matter if you can't see it. There's an iPad on your desk. So are you going to thank me for it or not?"

Holding a position of authority, whether as boss, parent, or pastor, doesn't give anyone the power to make someone believe something unless they have *reasons* to believe it.

Not only that, but "It's in the Bible, so believe it" won't help them when they run into people who tell them the Bible can't be trusted. "What, your mom told you to believe this? Your church didn't want you asking questions? You know what they were afraid of, don't you?"

Our kids need to know *why* they should believe what Christianity teaches. I can't tell you how crucial this is. (I'm devoting my entire career to it.) You'll find a list of resources for "Christianity and Truth" at the end of this book.

If we treat their questions as if there is something evil, wrong, or scary about asking, we cut them off from loving God with their minds—an essential part of the greatest commandment of all (Matt. 22:37). Their questions may seem risky but brushing them aside is riskier yet.

Celebrate Questions You Can't Answer!

What if they have a question you can't answer? Don't panic. Here's where you can really win with your teen! First, *celebrate* it, then *work the question* together. You might say something like, "Whoa, daughter, you stumped me with that one! We're going out for ice cream for that great question!" Would it surprise her to hear that from you? Would she love it? Of course! Would she come back the next day with something like, "Hey, Dad, how much does Jupiter weigh, and if you don't know the answer will you take me out for ice cream again?" My daughter would try that with me, I'm sure! Then it's time to clarify the rules: it has to be a question that matters, and it isn't going to be ice cream every time. I'm sure you get the picture, anyway.

No matter how you choose to celebrate your teen's hard questions, you'll find that treating them that way will encourage openness in your teen, strengthen your relationship, and give you a chance to research something together. You do need to take that final step, though. Don't just leave it there. Work through the question together. Use this book and the other resources recommended in it. Use the Internet. Ask your pastor or a good teacher. And explore together.

4. Explore Ideas Together

Whether you're dealing with issues that are unfamiliar to you or you're confident you already have all the answers, take the time to work through the issues with your teen. They'll benefit from the process, and you may find you have something to learn along the way as well.

Feel free to look at the skeptical side as well as the Christian answer. There's nothing to fear there. Some skeptical challenges might throw you off balance for a while, but I can assure you of this: if you keep at it, you'll find something secure and stable that you can grab on to from the Christian side, with solid evidences and reasoning behind it. I've been interacting with atheists online for more than ten years, and they've never put a question to me that I couldn't find a good answer for. And I really do mean a *good* answer, with evidence behind it, and reasonable, rational thinking running all the way through it. (Meanwhile, in almost every case I've found the atheists' and skeptics' challenges to be riddled with rational holes.)[2]

Let's consider an example. Your teen son comes home from school and says, "We have to stop discriminating against gays. It's causing too many suicides." You could answer, "That's not the issue: homosexuality is still wrong." You would be right, or at least mostly right.

---

2. See Tom Gilson and Carson Weitnauer, eds., *True Reason: Confronting the Irrationality of the New Atheism* (Grand Rapids: Kregel, 2014).

Or you could say, "That's all nonsense, made up by activists pushing the gay agenda." Would that be right, too?

I'm going to leave that question hanging, because at this point there's an even more important question for you to consider: *If you answered either of those ways, would your son believe you?* He might—for now. Someday, though, he's going to need to be able to explain why he believes what he does. When that day comes, "Mom told me" won't get him very far.

Suppose instead you answered, "Now, that's an interesting opinion. If people are committing suicide, that's tragic. Tell me, though, how do you know it's true? Can we look up some things on that together?" If you responded that way, he could learn at least three things, the first two of which would get through to him even before you even clicked into your web browser. First, not everything he hears is true. Second, you respect him enough to take his question seriously. Third, it's important that he know how to do his own research.

An example for research together

I just ran my own private practice session to see how that research might come out. I did a Google search on three key terms: *bullied gays suicide.* The first link that came up said, "Two out of every five victims of homophobic bullying contemplate suicide."

I noticed that the article said, "The survey, carried out for Stonewall—the pro-gay pressure group—by researchers at Cambridge University, urges the Government to adopt a series of measures to combat homophobia in schools."[3] That's just the kind of thing I would be looking for as a parent: an opportunity to talk with my teen about how to read these kinds of articles. In this case there's a glaring instance of research bias. So if I were with my son now (instead of writing here alone at my desk), I might ask, "Do you suppose if a tobacco company funded research on lung cancer, we would trust

---

3. Richard Garner, "Two Out of Every Five Victims of School Homophobic Bullying Contemplate Suicide, Says Survey," *Independent*, July 5, 2012, www.independent.co.uk/news/education/education-news/two-out-of-every-five-victims-of-school-homophobic-bullying-contemplate-suicide-says-survey-7917473.html.

the results without asking further questions?" I might suggest he try another Internet search: tobacco company funding cancer research. It's quite revealing. Research bias matters.

Reading through that article on gays, bullying, and suicide, I notice there are no comparison figures. Two out of five LGBT youth who are bullied consider suicide, it says. What about non-LGBT youth who are bullied? How many of them consider suicide? Is it two out of five for them, too? The article doesn't say. If the proportion is the same or higher among non-LGBT youth, then the article is guilty of an odd sort of bias in mentioning only LGBT cases. But if LGBT youth who are bullied contemplate suicide more than non-LGBT youth who are bullied, that would make me wonder what would cause the difference: why do LGBT students being bullied think about suicide more often than other, non-LGBT students who are also being bullied? What message does that send, and is it really what LGBT activists want us to pick up?

Either way, *can't we just agree that bullying is wrong, period?*

So what's the answer? What are the comparison numbers that the article doesn't include? Was the research really biased by its pro-gay funding source? I'll let you look that up for yourself. It's good practice, and besides, my purpose here isn't to address those questions. My point is to illustrate how we can work with our teens to help them evaluate the information they're running into, not only online, but almost everywhere they go.

Be cautious, by the way: there are some "Christian" answers that really aren't Christian at all. The Westboro Church is a good (bad) example. If you start with the resources I recommend in the Resource Guide, though, you'll be on reliable biblical territory.

5. Watch Out for Land Mines

These issues can be very personal, sometimes in ways you don't know. You can trip over land mines: unknown factors that can make a seemingly safe discussion blow up unexpectedly.

Suppose you're talking with your son, Jason. Jason has a good friend named Michael. They both go to your church, they've attended the same schools all their lives, and they've always been best friends. But Michael has seemed different lately, and you've been thinking he might be wondering about his sexuality. Jason knows more than you do about that: he knows that Michael has decided he's gay. Their classmates know, too. Jason has seen them harassing him over it, both at school and at church. He knows how much it's hurting Michael.

Into this situation, you drop one of the questions I suggested at the beginning of this chapter: "Do your friends think of Christians as being anti-gay?"

How do you think your son would respond? Chances are, his answer will have more to do with Michael than with what the Bible says—and that's not entirely wrong.

Yes, there could be *something* wrong about it, especially if your son lets Michael's experience trump God's truth in his mind. It's good, though, for him to talk freely about his friend and what he's going through. You would want to support him in that. Otherwise the conversation might blow up on you.

That's not the only potential land mine in a teen's life. There's pressure from school, from media, from other friends and acquaintances, even the irrational pressure of thinking that standing against gay rights is old-fashioned—that it belongs to your generation, not theirs.

You can defuse these kinds of potential explosions by responding, not reacting or escalating the tension. Just acknowledge the situation for what it is, and keep on listening.[4]

---

4. It might also be that your teen is asking questions about his or her own sexuality. That raises an entirely different set of heartbreaking questions and troubling issues. If that information comes out in the course of your conversations, I encourage you to seek counsel from someone whose approach combines grace with truth, who is well-informed by the Scriptures, and who has the benefit of long experience. To say more than that to such a complicated and emotionally fraught situation is beyond the scope of this book.

CHAPTER SEVEN
Relating to Friends

We're up to Generation Z now. The Millennials (Generation Y) are in the workforce. Our teens own the next letter in the alphabet. I wonder what my grandchildren's generation will be called, now that there are no letters left for them!

The word on Generation Z is that they're more pessimistic than Gen Y. They've been heavily influenced by school violence, and many of them have never known a time when the United States was not at war. Yet they're inspired by stories of rising above danger: think *Hunger Games*. They're realistic in matters like debt and spending, and security is an issue. They're constantly connected with their friends, and they think multitasking is for real so they're running at a fast pace. They eagerly embrace diversity. Socialization is constant yet distant, by way of technology.[1]

As with Gen X and Gen Y before them, this generation's network of friends is paramount. Actually, that's likely been true of youth ever since they began leaving the family shop or farm and discovering a world of their own. That's how I remember my own teenage years.

---

1. For most of that information, I could footnote my wife and myself as sources; we see it in our own two children. But there are others who agree. See, e.g., Emily Anatole, "Generation Z: Rebels with a Cause," *Forbes*, May 28, 2013, www.forbes.com/sites/onmarketing/2013/05/28/generation-z-rebels-with-a-cause/.

Sure, I had plenty of interests, mostly relating to school and music, but my friendships were deep and our connections frequent. Friendships have always mattered. For Generation Z, technology matters, too. Connections matter. Media (film, TV, YouTube, etc.) matters. Even in a culture that promotes diversity, fitting in matters. Technology allows friendships to be spread broadly (and thinly), which means young people can easily find a niche to fit into. If they're in public school, though, they can't avoid being influenced by, and caring about, what the rest of their world thinks and believes. This includes being influenced by their generation's overwhelming support for homosexuality, bisexuality, and increasingly also transgenderism. A 2013 NPR report drives the story home:

> Michael Dimock, director of Pew Research Center for the People and the Press, tells Don Gonyea, host of weekends on *All Things Considered*, that the pace at which millennials back gay marriage has rarely been matched.
>
> "You saw radical transformations in American attitudes about race in the '60s, '70s and '80s," Dimock says, "this isn't inherently unprecedented, but for the past decade or so this is certainly one of the biggest shifts we've seen."
>
> That shift also extends to young conservatives and those that identify as Republicans, Dimock says, a group whose support for same-sex marriage has nearly doubled in the past 10 years.
>
> "The trajectory is happening across party lines [and] across religious lines," he says.[2]

The youth I'm describing here aren't just "out there" somewhere. These are your teens, or at least they are your teens' friends. There's a good chance your teens' friends or classmates include gay, lesbian,

---

2. NPR Staff, "Millenials and Same-Sex Marriage: A Waning Divide," March 24, 2013, www.npr.org/2013/03/24/175201923/millennials-and-same-sex -marriage-a-waning-divide.

or transgender students. In 2008 (the most recent such study I could find), cnsnews.com reported:

> The Gay, Lesbian and Straight Education Network says based on the results of a new poll, about 5 percent of American high school students "identify as gay or lesbian"; 16 percent said they have a homosexual relative; and 72 percent said they know someone who is homosexual.[3]

It's not likely those numbers have decreased since then. If your child is in public school, it's very likely he or she knows, or is friends with, an openly LGBT classmate. It's even more certain that most of your teen's friends think it's wrong to oppose homosexuality or gay marriage, and they're influencing your teen with their opinions. When we ask our teens to stand with biblical beliefs on this, we're asking them to stand practically alone.

It's the hardest thing we could ask of them.

How *can* we ask it of them, then? Because we have to, if we're going to raise them in the knowledge of the truth and help launch them into a lifetime of following Jesus Christ. Anything less would be giving in to the world's ways, ways that lead to death.

So we must. But again, how? I believe there are five steps we must follow to prepare them to withstand peer pressure, stand with the truth, and display the love of Christ.

1. Build Intrinsic Strength

A teen has to have her own strength to carry her through the day. Her parents' convictions won't do it for her. We need to explain what we believe and why we believe it. Then we need to follow through with our teens as they seek to develop their own convictions.

---

3. Susan Jones, "Poll: Five Percent of High School Students 'Identify as Gay,'" July 7, 2008, cnsnews.com/news/article/poll-five-percent-high-school-students -identify-gay.

2. Provide External Support

Your teen needs to connect with other teens who don't think he's homophobic or crazy. He needs a vibrant, biblically based, seriously Bible-studying youth group. He doesn't need more pizza, at least, not that much more pizza. If your church's youth group isn't grappling with what we believe and why, you might want to find another one that is. Teens need a safe place to work out how to live life in this difficult culture. Home is paramount, but church comes in close behind it. Like home, church should be a place where the truth is known and taught with conviction, yet students are free to work through their questions without being shut down.

3. Teach an Attitude of Love, Respect, and Friendship

If your teen has bought into your convictions, she might have a reputation around school of being homophobic. Later in this book we'll talk about what's wrong with that word. For now, though, the best defense is also the best witness: to love LGBT classmates with the love of Christ, to be gracious in disagreement, and to be firm in conviction. My favorite reference on this is Colossians 4:5–6: "Walk in wisdom toward outsiders, making the best use of the time. Let your speech always be gracious, seasoned with salt, so that you may know how you ought to answer each person." The *New Bible Commentary* explains,

> *Seasoned with salt* meant "witty" in pagan usage but here suggests language that is not dull or flat but is interesting and well chosen (the rabbis sometimes used "salt" to mean "wisdom"). Christians need to respond with the right word to those who ask questions, perhaps in connection with their beliefs and behaviour. The response should be appropriate (*cf.* 1 Pet. 3:15): "every one is to be treated as an end in himself and not subjected to a stock harangue."[4]

---

4. G. B. Caird in *New Bible Commentary*, 21st century ed., ed. G. J. Wenham, J. A. Motyer, D. A. Carson, and R. T. France (Downers Grove, IL: InterVarsity Press, 1994).

Our daughter has had more than one gay friend at the college she attends. We're okay with that. We were okay with her having LGBT friends in high school.[5] We're okay with it now, as we were then, because we had prepared her in the knowledge and training I've been talking about in this chapter, and we know she knows how to stand for what's true. We get our instruction on that from 1 Corinthians 5:9–12:

> I wrote to you in my letter not to associate with sexually immoral people—not at all meaning the sexually immoral of this world, or the greedy and swindlers, or idolaters, since then you would need to go out of the world. But now I am writing to you not to associate with anyone who bears the name of brother if he is guilty of sexual immorality or greed, or is an idolater, reviler, drunkard, or swindler—not even to eat with such a one. For what have I to do with judging outsiders? Is it not those inside the church whom you are to judge?

If the topic of sexual morality or gay marriage comes up in conversation, a Christian teen should be prepared, equipped, and willing to speak the truth in love. There's no need for it to come up in every conversation, though; and when it's not being discussed, there's usually no need to make it an issue. Rather, it's an opportunity to show the love of Christ—while also demolishing stereotypes—by treating the other person as a friend. A Christian student should find it natural to enjoy conversation with LGBT classmates, to study together, to invite them to sit at lunch with them—in short, to be a friend, provided the discussion doesn't veer off into immorality (which, by the way, can be an even more frequent issue with straight classmates).

I can think of one major exception to this friendship principle: if you think your teen is questioning his or her gender identity or sexual orientation, it would be wise to protect your teen from persons

---

5. Our son attended a very small public school where, to our knowledge, there were no gay or lesbian students.

who would encourage him or her to adopt the alternative sexual life-style that he or she is wondering about.

Of course it goes without saying that same-sex friendships are a great idea, and same-sex outings are an important and healthy part of growing up; but if you catch a hint that it's anything like a same-sex *date*, then it's time to step in and say no. As long as they're living in your home, or even while you're paying for their college education, you can enforce that rule.

What About "Hate the Sin, Love the Sinner"?

Should you be teaching your teen to relate to LGBT classmates by "hating the sin, loving the sinner"? Yes and no.

We're all sinners (Rom. 3:23; 1 John 1). That's the first thing to bear in mind.

Beyond that, I'm not big on one-liners. They're frequently thought-less and often offensive. All of part 3 of this book is about answering gay-rights one-liners. LGBT people hear the one-liner "hate the sin, love the sinner," and (typically) find it impossible to take seriously. They don't believe it's possible for us to love them while rejecting their sexual orientation, so for them it's nothing better than a cute saying—cute, and yet not very honest.

So this slogan's value is slight. I wouldn't use it in public, and I wouldn't teach it to my kids. The *concept* behind the slogan has life, however, if we think it through to its logical conclusions. One way to do that is to run it in reverse. If LGBT people say that calling them wrong means we're hating them, they're building a trap that's bound to catch them, too. They call *us* wrong, after all. If calling someone wrong means you hate them, then that means they must be haters, too.

Very, very few LGBT people (maybe none) would want to be con-sidered haters. Most of them *aren't* haters. My point here certainly isn't to show that they are; it's to show that it's possible to disagree deeply without being hateful. LGBT persons do it all the time. If they can consider our words or actions wrong without hating us, then why couldn't we consider their words or actions wrong, too, without hating them? So we really can hate the sin and love the sinner, even though I don't recommend phrasing it that way.

Notice, by the way, that I showed that "hate the sin, love the sinner" is valid, without even mentioning the Bible. If we can do that, how much more can we demonstrate it using the Bible! God set the example: he abhors sin, yet he loves us. We who follow Christ by the power of the Holy Spirit, being "partakers of the divine nature" (2 Peter 1:4) can do the same. We can't do it perfectly, but the more we grow in Christ the more we can gain his power, reflect his character, and go beyond human limitations.

It's not impossible after all. Still, *the slogan has got to go*; it just stirs up too much emotion.

4. Encourage Concern for Bullying

Look up "LGBT bullying" on the Internet, and you'll be flooded with tragic stories of students contemplating or committing suicide, dropping out of school, and more. Your teen can show the love of Christ by standing up for those who are being pushed around. In the Bible, the usual word for "pushed around" is *oppressed*, but it's the same idea, and God is always on the side of those who suffer that way. That doesn't mean he sides with everyone's moral choices. It does mean that he hates the strong picking on the weak. Christian teens should have the strongest reputation in school for standing up against anti-LGBT bullying.

5. Jump in Where Needed

Your child needs you to stay in touch with what's happening at school. I speak from experience: both of our children were bullied. There was one especially violent incident for which we probably should have pressed charges against a classmate.

Your teen may not be getting physically bullied for her beliefs, but shunned or shamed instead. Either way, we parents need to keep in touch with whatever might be going on. Our teens need our coaching and guidance. They need our advice on how to stand up for themselves. They might need us to ask a counselor or administrator to step in on their behalf.

This isn't easy. In our family, we did some of it well and some of it poorly. I know this for sure: if we had not been involved, we wouldn't have done any of it well.

CHAPTER EIGHT

Relating to Teachers, Administrators, and Professors

Do you know what your college-bound teen is heading into? My two kids are in college and beyond, and I've been a national field director and vice president with Ratio Christi, a campus apologetics ministry. I can tell you from experience, colleges today are oppressive toward biblical morality.

I'll give you just two examples out of many that I could share. At the University of North Carolina, Wilmington, in 2014, graduates going to their commencement ceremony could wear "a gold cord for good grades, a purple one for being a homosexual, and a lavender one for just being really supportive of homosexuals."[1] That's not just being supportive; that's promoting homosexuality in the highest degree.

Not long ago I took a walk around the campus of the College of William & Mary in Virginia, observing the advertisements posted on bulletin boards. It was gay pride week, with dozens of sexually charged events scheduled in support. A sex show, unrelated to gay pride week, was coming to campus not long after.

---

1. Mike Adams, "Three Cords and the Truth," June 10, 2014, Townhall.com, townhall .com/columnists/mikeadams/2014/06/10/three-cords-and-the-truth-n1849498 /page/full.

As I'm writing this I'm checking online, where William & Mary's online diversity portal today has an event listed under the title "Transgender Ally 101 Workshop." The college describes it as an opportunity to "Join us to learn some of the basics about transgender identities and everyday actions you can take to be respectful and an ally."[2] (I searched in vain for a workshop on how to be respectful toward evangelical Christians.)

Thankfully "diversity" hasn't reached that extreme in most middle or high schools. Still it's not unusual to find schools supporting LGBT initiatives including the "Day of Silence" coordinated by GLSEN—the Gay, Lesbian & Straight Education Network. The Day of Silence is student-led but involves administration cooperation. The Gay-Straight Alliance (GSA) claims to have clubs on 53 percent of California high school campuses.

Statistics of that sort aren't your main concern as a parent, though. What you're concerned about is your own child's experience at school. Schools vary widely. Some schools allow boys to use girls' restrooms if they consider themselves girls. Some teach stories of families with two dads or two moms. Vancouver, BC, schools just implemented gender-neutral pronouns—*xe*, *xem*, and *xyr*—that transgender students may request teachers and staff use with them.[3] A California law went into effect on January 1, 2012, requiring the inclusion of the contributions of various groups in the history of California and the United States. This section already included men and women and numerous ethnic groups; the expanded language now includes (additions in bold):

> . . . a study of the role and contributions of both men and women, Native Americans, African Americans, Mexican **Americans**, Asian **Americans**, Pacific Islanders, **European**

2. William & Mary "Diversity Events" listed for November 19, 2014, accessed November 4, 2014, events.wm.edu/calendar/day/diversity/2014/11/19.

3. Joseph Brean, "Vancouver School Board's Genderless Pronouns—Xe, Xem, Xyr—Not Likely to Stick, if History Is Any Indication," June 17, 2014, National Post, news.nationalpost.com/2014/06/17/vancouver-school-boards-genderless-pronouns-not-likely-to-stick-if-history-is-any-indication/?__federated=1.

Americans, lesbian, gay, bisexual, and transgender Americans, persons with disabilities, and members of other ethnic **and cultural** groups, to the economic, political, and social development of California and the United States of America, with particular emphasis on portraying the role of these groups in contemporary society.[4]

The same law also prohibits any policy that would exclude textbooks from schools for promoting LGBT values.

As I write this, we have yet to see what changes may come following federal approval of gay marriage. Count on this, though: things are bound to get more challenging, not less.

Pressures at School: Coaching for Students

It could be that your student is experiencing no gay rights–related pressure from teachers or staff. If so, this chapter may be of little interest to you. If, however, your school places your child under LGBT-related pressures, I hope to provide both you and your teen a few good ways to approach teachers and administrators. I'll begin by suggesting ways you can coach your teen to respond, and then I'll take a look at what parents can do on campus.

Know What Students' Rights Are

Students have every right to talk about their faith at school. The National Education Association's own pro-LGBT training guide for teachers and staff says,

> Are people entitled to express religious or moral opposition to the LGBT community?

> Yes. Within the school context, however, students have more

---

4. "Frequently Asked Questions: Senate Bill 48," California Department of Education, accessed June 28, 2014, www.cde.ca.gov/ci/cr/cf/senatebill48faq.asp; emphasis in original.

limited free speech rights. Student speech can be prohibited if it is likely to cause a substantial disruption of school activities or create a hostile educational environment. Epithets [name-calling], slurs, and harassment fall outside the free speech protection.[5]

Ironically, that document uses the hostile epithet *homophobic* seven times.

Teens can express their religious beliefs quite freely as long as they don't harass, bully, or call people names, which Christians shouldn't want to do anyway.

The Alliance Defending Freedom (ADF), a legal group specializing in religious freedom, says every student can:

- Pray at school
- Talk about God in class assignments
- Start a religious club on campus that receives the same rights and resources as other clubs
- Freely share his or her faith with other students[6]

Further, you can opt your children out of curriculum that requires them to violate your family's religious beliefs.[7] The ADF goes into much more expert legal advice in an online FAQ document I suggest you study.[8] Their website also includes information on college students' rights.

---

5. "Strengthening the Learning Environment: A School Employee's Guide to Gay, Lesbian, Bisexual, and Transgender Issues," prepared by Robert Kim and Kevin K. Kumashiro, 2nd ed. (Washington, DC: National Education Association, 2006), p. 12, www.nea.org/assets/docs/glbtstrenghtenlearningenvirong2006.pdf.

6. "While Attending Public School, Your Child Can," accessed June 21, 2014, Alliance Defending Freedom, www.alliancedefendingfreedom.org/issues/public-education/k-thru-12.

7. Ibid.

8. See www.alliancedefendingfreedom.org/content/docs/issues/school/FAQ-Religious-Freedom-in-Public-Schools.pdf.

Be Wise with Faculty

Rights aren't all that matter. Having rights doesn't mean it's always a good idea to mount a direct battle. I'm not talking about avoiding anything; this is about coaching your children to be wise.

Chapter 4 of Greg Koukl's brilliant book *Tactics: A Game Plan for Discussing Your Christian Convictions* includes good advice that's intended for college students, but is just as fitting for middle or high schoolers: "Never make a frontal assault on a superior force in an entrenched position."[9] Translation: *You're the student, they're the teacher (or the staff person). They have firepower you don't have. Don't attack head-on. You'll get steamrolled.*

That doesn't mean students shouldn't stand up for what's right. It means there are better and worse ways to do that, and a head-on assault is usually a worse way. Suppose the teacher tells the class that everyone should be tolerant of homosexuality. A student could raise her hand and say, "No, that's not right! My religion says it's wrong." Probably the best thing that could happen would be her teacher retreating to something like, "Well, I know not everyone agrees on that." (That's the *best* thing. I don't want to think about what else could happen.) Then what? Too often the next words out of the teacher's mouth would be, "Class, stop laughing; it's impolite!" Directly contradicting a teacher usually gets a student nowhere.

Questions are better, especially something like this: "Teacher, could you please explain what you mean by that?" Once the teacher answers, the student can move on to follow-up questions like, "How did you come to that conclusion?" and even, "If people don't agree with that, shouldn't we be tolerant of them, too?"

The teacher might try to put her on the spot and ask, "Okay, then, apparently you're one of those behind-the-times religious people who disagrees. What do you believe, and what makes you think you're right?"

The student could take that as an opportunity to witness for Jesus

---

9. Gregory Koukl, *Tactics: A Game Plan for Discussing Your Christian Convictions* (Grand Rapids: Zondervan, 2009), 66.

Christ, but success is doubtful: it's not likely the teacher would let her get anywhere with it. The timing is all wrong. Instead, she should make a strategic retreat: "I'm not the teacher here, and I haven't brought up my religion at all. I just wanted to hear you explain what you were saying." That tactic puts the teacher on the spot instead of the student.

The student could go on with questions of that sort for as long as the teacher seemed willing to answer them. Another follow-up question might be, "I'm not sure I understand your answer. It still makes me wonder why tolerance is for certain groups and not for others."

I wouldn't coach my teen to press too hard, though. This takes skill. It isn't easy to come up with the right question at the right time, and ask it with the right tone of respectfulness. Not every teacher is open to a discussion going down that road. The wise student knows when to back off.

Be Wise with Administrators

That advice is for the classroom. With higher-level school personnel it's different. If my child were to run into opposition from her school's administrators, I'd want her to back down politely for the moment and then get her mom and me involved. That's not cowardly; it's wise. Even if your child is right and the administrator is wrong, a conflict between a student and an administrator is either (a) an unfair fight on the administrator's part, or (b) really poor strategy on the student's part.

Our Christian convictions don't require us to press on in circumstances like that. A student's witness is better served by being both respectful and wise.

Pressures at School: Advice for Parents

Believe it or not—and I hope it isn't that hard to believe—the administration at your teen's school can be your best resource, even your "best friend." You can gain a lot by cultivating a positive relationship with school staff members.

My wife and I have learned that from experience, not LGBT-related but instructive nonetheless, since the principle I'm speaking of applies to all kinds of issues. We're the only parents I know whose son was sent to the vice-principal's office, and someone got suspended—and it was the vice-principal, not the student. (Actually, I have no *official* word that he was suspended, but we know he was absent the next five school days.) We happened to be on campus for unrelated reasons that day. We saw our son coming out of that meeting. He looked dazed. He told us quite seriously, "I'm never coming back to this school again." When we heard what had just gone on (strictly verbal in nature, but definitely wrong), we agreed with him. The next morning we started homeschooling him. He was in eighth grade at the time.

We had some things to work through with higher-level school district officials after that, as you can imagine. We got to know the school superintendent very well. I can't tell you all that we discussed because we agreed not to share it publicly. I can say this much, though. We treated him with genuine respect and courtesy, even in the midst of hard conversations. He ended up providing us the right kind of help. And when I ran into him in a restaurant a few years later, he greeted me as a friend.

That was just the most extreme of many encounters we had with administrators. One of our daughter's elementary school teachers decided to crack down on discipline—which had been a yearlong problem—by placing a mark on the blackboard next to students' names every time they acted up. One student got twenty-two marks in one day. That's a lot of acting up! Amazingly, the teacher disciplined our daughter for counting those twenty-two marks. That same "high-mark" student liked to shoot staples ("hornets," he called them) with a rubber band. One "hornet" narrowly missed a girl's eye. What did the teacher do? She put a mark next to his name on the board.

This kind of thing went on for weeks. We went to the principal. We knew him already, and that made all the difference. He moved our daughter to another classroom.

Our relationships with administrators were almost always positive. One time we offered to donate a Bible-based set of Accelerated Reader tests to our daughter's elementary school. After weeks of waiting for an okay from the school district's attorneys, the principal gladly accepted it.

The key to it all, I think, was something I said in one of our meetings with the school superintendent. "Dr. S——," I said, "I want to make sure we're not misleading you. You'll find as we meet with you that we'll be very cordial, very polite, very professional—and also *very persistent*." We knew our rights, and we meant to have them honored, by all appropriate means possible. But we weren't going to ruin our Christian witness by being rude about it.

Granted, those incidents weren't directly tied to morality or religious freedom, but they illustrate the benefits of building positive relationships with administrators in case something goes wrong in your teen's school experience.

We did have one instance that was directly connected to our faith. Our daughter's middle-school history teacher told the class that Christianity was "a myth, like all the other religions." We had already established a good relationship with that school's principal by volunteering at the school and by having had a friendly meeting or two with him. So when we informed him of this irregularity, he was happy to arrange a meeting for us with the teacher.

The school district was apparently more nervous about us than he was. They brought someone in from the district office "to observe." We had a friendly conversation, the teacher apologized, he told us he had already corrected what he had said in class, we shook hands and left.

All this adds up to one general recommendation: get to know your child's teachers and administrators. When a conflict comes up, you might be able to settle it in a completely friendly manner.

If, however, the cordial, personal approach doesn't work, don't escalate the dispute into nastiness. Instead, take a close look at the ADF's FAQ sheet I mentioned earlier, the one that explains your children's rights in public school. Stand firmly yet calmly with those rights.

If you need legal help on a matter relating to your child's religious freedom at school, contact the Alliance Defending Freedom (www.alliancedefendingfreedom.org). They'll determine whether your case appears to have merit. If it does, they'll probably send a simple letter, and that may be all it will take to settle it for you. They don't generally charge for this service. If the letter doesn't settle it and you need more direct legal help, they may provide that for free, too.

Choose Your Battles

The old saying goes, "you can't win 'em all." Actually in the end Christ does win them all: he is the forever conquering King. In the meantime, though, you may find that "you can't even fight 'em all." In some schools (not yours, I hope, but some) the battles may be too many to keep up with, and you'll have to let some of them go.

If that's your situation, I recommend you focus on two kinds of battles: those that you can definitely win, like the one I mentioned with my daughter's history teacher; and those that you *must* fight whether or not you win. If your child is being asked to support immorality, you must fight that. Whether that battle is winnable hardly matters: if you don't stand for what's right your child will conclude that morality isn't very important to you. Some things are worth fighting for, no matter what.

Always take your stand in Christ's way, though. Your teen is watching and learning from you, and you're representing Christ to the school. Remember the biblical principles summarized in chapter 5. Stand your ground with truth, love, and strength, whether or not you see any hope of winning.

What About the "Day of Silence"?

One further issue still needs attention: the annual "Day of Silence" on behalf of bullied gay and lesbian students, observed in schools all across the country, sponsored by GLSEN, the Gay, Lesbian & Straight Education Network. Students agree not to speak for a day to bring attention to LGBT bullying. A sample "speaking card" on the Day of Silence website reads,

Please understand my reasons for not speaking today. I am participating in the Day of Silence (DOS), a national youth movement bringing attention to the silence faced by lesbian, gay, bisexual and transgender people and their allies. My deliberate silence echoes that silence, which is caused by anti-LGBT bullying, name-calling and harassment. I believe that ending the silence is the first step toward building awareness and making a commitment to address these injustices.

Think about the voices you ARE NOT hearing today.[10]

Students who don't go along stick out like noisy monkeys. Peer pressure can be powerful. Besides, it's a day to stand against bullying LGBT students, and who's not against bullying?

I've seen two good strategies in response. (I'm sure there are others.) The first is to support the anti-bullying message without focusing on the LGBT side of it. Your child could use T-shirts, signs, or other ways of showing she's against *all* bullying, including LGBT but not only LGBT. That's a perfectly legitimate way of expressing her beliefs.

The second strategy I would recommend is the "Day of Dialogue," which Focus on the Family promotes as "a free-speech initiative that creates a safe place for public school students to exercise their religious freedoms and express their deeply held Christian beliefs in a loving and respectful manner."[11] Why should silence be better than dialogue, anyway?

Again, the idea is to stand up for what you know is right, to confront what needs confronting, and to do it in a respectful, cordial manner. Always remember Colossians 4:5–6: "Walk in wisdom toward outsiders, making the best use of the time. Let your speech always be gracious, seasoned with salt, so that you may know how you ought to answer each person."

---

10. "GLSEN Day of Silence," Gay, Lesbian & Straight Education Network, accessed July 1, 2014, www.dayofsilence.org/PDFs/dos_palmcard.pdf.

11. "Day of Dialogue," Focus on the Family, accessed June 21, 2014, www.dayof dialogue.com. See also www.focusonthefamily.com/socialissues/education /day-of-dialogue/day-of-dialogue.

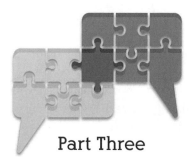

Part Three

PRACTICAL HELP IN HANDLING THE CHALLENGES

PART 3: PRACTICAL HELP IN HANDLING THE CHALLENGES

The majority of gay-rights rhetorical strategies are short on substance, and long on imagery, slogans, and what I call *stingers*: quick one-line shots with barbs on them that can hurt if we let them. These challenges are pithy, and they can seem powerful. Like a lion roaring right in your face at the 3-D movie theater, they might look threatening, but when we take off the reality-distorting glasses we find them to be flat, blurry, and unimpressive.

These challenges are intended to put us on the defensive, if not completely on the run. Their purpose is to make us look uncaring, unthinking, and disconnected from reality. On another level, their purpose is to drive a wedge between your teen and his faith in Christ, or at least his confidence in the moral teachings of the faith. This is not only about rhetoric, in other words.

Is there a way to protect our teens and ourselves from being taken in by this faux 3-D rhetoric? That's what the rest of this book is for. It's a practical, parent-friendly, topic-by-topic look at major anti-Christian LGBT talking points, with answers.

I don't try to say everything that could be said on these topics, so if you or your teen want to explore deeper, the resource guide at the back of the book will direct you to more information on these subjects. Most of the time, though, I think you'll find the answers here sufficient.

Here's how this part of the book is organized. There are twenty-seven topics, each of them an LGBT challenge, slogan, or talking point meant to undermine traditional values or Christian belief. Under each topic there are four parts. "The Challenge" explains briefly what gay-rights proponents are trying to get across. "Truths Your Teen Needs to Know" serves as a short introductory response to that challenge. "Digging Deeper" is where I explain the issue in greater depth. Finally, "Tips for Talking with Your Teen" provides you with a sample of what you can say as you speak with your teen. It doesn't come in the form of scripts to follow, but rather as guides for what you could say while dialoguing with your teen.

An Overarching Word of Wisdom

Sometimes people will try to entice us into a position where they can label us as bigots. Greg Koukl has this extremely helpful advice for those situations:

> If you're placed in a situation where you suspect your convictions will be labeled intolerant, bigoted, narrow-minded, or judgmental, then turn the tables. When someone asks for your personal views about a moral issue, preface your remarks with a question.
>
> Say, "You know, this is actually a very personal question you're asking. I don't mind answering, but before I do, I want to know if it's safe to offer my views. So let me ask you a question: Do you consider yourself a tolerant person or an intolerant person? Is it safe to give my opinion, or are you going to judge me for my point of view? Do you respect diverse points of view, or do you condemn others for convictions that differ from your own?"[1]

If they answer that they respect diverse points of view, you can hold them to that. If they condemn you for your position, you can gently remind them what they just told you: they aren't the kind of person who would do that.

Always help your teens remember you're encouraging them to listen, understand, and trust God for the right time to respond when they hear this challenge. Speaking the truth is vital; speaking it at the right time, and with the right relational connection established, are also vital.

I've divided these topics into three groups. The first one deals with Christians' so-called intolerance and hate. The second group has to do with social policy, and the third is about challenges related to our belief in God and the Bible.

---

1. Greg Koukl, "How to Get Out of a Corner," *Stand to Reason*, July 16, 2014, www .str.org/articles/how-to-get-out-of-a-corner-2#.VHy1H76e-ZY.

GROUP A: REGARDING INTOLERANCE AND HATE

Christianity's reputation isn't all good these days. Teens are frequently forced to deal with accusations that Christians are hateful, intolerant, bigoted, and other not very nice things.

We want our teens to be able to stand for their beliefs confidently, graciously, and lovingly. That isn't always easy for you and me. Think how much harder it must be for our kids! The topics in this group will give you what you need to guide them toward gracious and confident responses, as they stand up for belief in Jesus Christ and biblical standards of morality.

"You're a hater."

The Challenge
"You're against gay rights. That means you're a hater."

Truths Your Teen Needs to Know
Yes, some people oppose gay rights out of hatred. If that's the case for your teen, a family review of the gospel of grace would be a good idea. Otherwise, as we'll see below, anyone who says this about your teen is probably guilty of stereotyping, which is one of the few things almost everyone still agrees is really wrong. This charge also makes the mistake of assuming disagreement equals hate.

Digging Deeper
When someone tells us we're haters, chances are they're basing that on a stereotype, not on who we really are. Sure, if we've demonstrated hate, that's one thing, but few Christians actually do that.

Where does the *hater* charge come from, then? It's common for gay-rights activists to accuse us of hating them simply because we don't agree with them. When they do that, though, they're disagreeing with us, too. If disagreement meant hate, then they, too, would be haters, for the very same reason they use to pin the *hater* label on us. As for stereotyping, you'll find what I mean by that when you read "Tips for Talking with Your Teen" below. In our world of political correctness, stereotyping is one of our culture's few remaining big "sins." If they're stereotyping, we can point it out to them and thus defuse the *hater* label without being defensive about it.

Tips for Talking with Your Teen

The answer I'm suggesting you share with your teen here is in three parts. The first part might be the only one you need to use; the other two are available if you need them. You might say something like this to your teen, always bearing in mind that this isn't a script; it's a guide for discussion:

1. Stereotyping

It doesn't feel good to be called a hater, does it? People can hurt you with language like that. Maybe you can help them realize it's not true, by answering this way:

You've decided I'm a hater, but I don't think you really know me well enough to know whether I am or not. How about if we sit down together and talk? After we spend some time talking, if you still think I'm a hater, then you might have the right to say so. Until then, you're saying it without knowing me. When someone makes a judgment like that without knowing a person, they've probably reached that conclusion by stereotyping. So tell me, please: do you really believe in stereotyping other people?

Of course you know that as parents we only want you to do this with people you really should be hanging out with, like classmates and other teens. If it's an older adult, you might be better off just ignoring what they say, since it may not even matter that much what they think of you.

If it really does matter, like if it's a friend's parent, I'd rather you get me involved. I'd probably go to that parent and ask them the same thing I've just suggested you ask your friend. I wouldn't want you to offer to get together with the person unless you really mean it. I'm not asking you to fake anything. If you do get together, though, it could give you the chance to help them overcome some stereotypes.

2. Disagreement Isn't Always Hate

Here's a question you could bring up, too: "How did you reach the conclusion that I'm a hater?" If they say it's because you don't agree with them about LGBT issues, you could ask, "Does disagreement always mean hate?"

Then you could also ask, "Have you noticed that you disagree with me? If my disagreeing with you means I'm a hater, why doesn't your disagreeing with me make you a hater? But honestly, I don't think you're a hater; I'm just trying to show that it's wrong to call anyone a hater just because they disagree."

3. Giving Reasons

Those two approaches might be all it takes to help your friend realize you're not a hater after all. Unfortunately some people will still push back anyway. They might say, "But you wouldn't disagree unless you were a hater. It's the only reason anyone would refuse to support LGBT!" That's when you could ask whether they want to hear your real reasons for your beliefs. If they refuse to hear you, they're probably stereotyping; that is, they're jumping to conclusions about you without listening to you. If so, it's okay to tell them that's what they're doing.

If they say they do want to listen to your reasons, you should be able to have a good conversation. I'd like to help you know those reasons better. How about if you read chapters 2 through 5, and especially the middle ones, three and four, in Critical Conversations? *Then let's talk about what you've learned there, and whether you agree that there really are good reasons that you could pass along to your friend.*

"You're homophobic."

The Challenge

"If you're against homosexuality or same-sex marriage, that means you're homophobic."

Truths Your Teen Needs to Know

Simply being opposed to something doesn't mean you have an irrational fear of it. Christians are opposed to casual divorce, but we don't fear people who get divorced. There is, however, a point where fear is rational and not phobic at all. We have reasonable grounds to be concerned over the damage LGBT activism could do in our culture.

Digging Deeper

Of all the stingers in part 3 of this book, this one is the most classic. It's short and it carries a bite.

It's also seriously distorted. The suffix *-phobia* refers to an irrational feeling of aversion, fear, or hatred toward something that a normal person would have no trouble with. Stick that label on a person, and suddenly he's carrying the stigma of psychological inferiority. He's abnormal. He's "filled with irrational fear." Get enough people repeating that message, and you've got a weapon with real rhetorical power working for you. That's what the label *homophobia* does: it classifies gay-rights opponents as psychological cripples.

It's no wonder activists like the term.

What is this supposed phobia, though? I'll use myself as an example. I've been to more than one party hosted by a gay friend of mine. Many of the other guests have been LGBT persons, and in each case, my friendship with the host was stronger after the event than before. That could hardly be the case if I had been afraid of the other guests, or if I had given any hint that I hated them. (If you're wondering whether there was anything weird going on at these parties, the answer is no, and *please be cautious of stereotypes*.) The fact is, I don't carry that kind of fear or hatred toward LGBT people.

Now, I'm willing to grant this much: I have a strong aversion to the idea of certain physical acts practiced by persons of the same sex. I think they're wrong, and I find the thought of them quite unpleasant. But that isn't what the accusation of "homophobia" usually seems to be about. Most often it's about our supposed fear or hatred of LGBT people.

Additionally, I'll admit to being concerned over what might happen to our country and the world as homosexuality takes hold as a moral norm. Sexual morality has a purpose: it's for the strengthening of families and the good of future generations (remember chapter 3). I fear the kind of damage that could realistically result from immorality being called morality, and wrong called right. That's no *phobia*, though. There's nothing irrational about fearing things that carry a genuine risk of real harm.

LGBT people and their supporters might disagree with that. Still it's unhelpful for them to label it as a phobia. When they medicalize our beliefs that way, they cut off dialogue. They close their ears. And remember from chapter 5 how they objected to their sexual orientations being labeled as psychiatric disorders? They've turned the tables and done the same to us!

Very few teens are genuinely afraid of LGBT persons, so "homophobia" probably doesn't fit most teens at all. If, however, there is some hint of it in our teens, it's probably something we parents need to explore in our own hearts, since our attitudes as parents will influence our teens' attitudes. The question starts with you and me: "Am I afraid of LGBT people, really?" or, "Do I harbor hatred in my heart toward them?"

If so, our teens might pick up that hatred from us. More likely these days our own children would find those beliefs repugnant. Either way we need to work through those feelings and beliefs before we can coach our children. This is the time to overcome that hatred or fear, if you feel that way toward LGBT persons. I would encourage you to spend time meditating on Scripture passages where the Word makes it clear that we're all sinners, all deserving of God's judgment, all caught up in our deadly flaws and failures. Study passages on forgiveness, especially the Lord's Prayer and what follows it in Matthew 6:7–15. If there is fear in your heart, read Psalm 23 along with John 10, and consider how Christ is the Good Shepherd who lays down his life for you. Pray that God would give you a loving, calm, peaceful heart.

And then try to find some LGBT person to befriend. Fear and hatred are fueled by lack of knowledge. Get to know someone as a friend, and those feelings are likely to fade away. Who knows? Depending on whom you make friends with, you might even have a part in helping them overcome their fear or hatred of Christians.

Tips for Talking with Your Teen

Some of what I wrote about stereotyping under the previous topic, "You're a hater," might fit here, since for the most part, labels like *homophobic* are stereotypes. Besides that, you might say something like this to your teen, always bearing in mind that this isn't a script; it's a guide for discussion:

Homophobia can mean many different things. Do you know what your friend means when they label you with that? Does your friend even know? How about if you find out, just by asking them, "What do you mean by that?"[1] *Let them really explain it to you, so you're not dealing with an empty label or mere name-calling. You might discover they can't even answer that question. They might be so used to labeling people that way, they've never taken the time to think through what it means!*

Whether they can answer you or not, the next question you might ask them is just as simple as the first one: "Okay, if that's what you think about me, how did you come to that conclusion?" You don't have to ask it in exactly those words. You could ask, for example, "What does homophobic *mean, in your opinion? What leads you to think I'm homophobic?"*

Then you really ought to listen. You've asked a question, after all, so you need to show you're genuinely interested in the answer. Then when

---

1. This question and the next one both come from Greg Koukl, *Tactics: A Game Plan for Discussing Your Christian Convictions* (Grand Rapids: Zondervan, 2009), 49ff.

the time comes, explain what phobia *really means: being irrationally afraid, or avoiding something for irrational reasons. Ask them, "Do I really look afraid of anyone here? Am I avoiding LGBT people? I'm not. So why are you labeling me as if I were?"*

It wouldn't be a bad idea to add this for your teen to think about, too:

You know, there was a time when LGBT people rose up and persuaded psychologists and psychiatrists that it really hurt them to pin a mental illness label on them. Don't you wonder why they've turned around and done the same thing to you and me?

"Why are you so intolerant?"

The Challenge
"You Christians won't accept other people's moral values. You think your morality is supposed to be everyone's morality. Why are you so intolerant?"

Truths Your Teen Needs to Know
Tolerance used to mean accepting other people's right to be who they are and believe what they believe. Frequently now, though, it means considering their opinions and values to be just as valid, good, and true as our own. That's impossible—not just for Christians, but for everybody. Tolerance is actually a counterfeit virtue that puts distance between people, unlike real virtues like respect and love that can bring people together.

Digging Deeper
Today's so-called tolerance is a weak, counterfeit virtue, and impossible besides.

It's impossible because no one can think all ideas are equally true, valid, and good. The person who tells us, "You're intolerant!" is telling us our opinions are bad and shameful. That is, he doesn't consider our ideas to be just as true, valid, and good as his own. By his own definition, therefore, when he calls us intolerant, he can't help but be intolerant himself!

Even if it weren't impossible, the modern form of intolerance would still be a weak virtue, as virtues go. Suppose I'm tolerant (in today's sense) of someone else's music, clothing style, or habits. All that really means is I'm not going to complain about them. If I'm tolerant of someone's religious views, it means I'll silently let them believe what they want to believe, even though I think they're wrong.

Notice how this kind of tolerance creates distance between people. It's all about refusing to disagree openly, keeping our own beliefs and values hidden behind a wall of noncommunication, even pretense.

We have to keep *ourselves* walled off and hidden. There's no authenticity there, no true human connection, just distant silence. Is there a stronger virtue than tolerance? Yes. There's *genuine respect*, as in, "I respect you enough to expect you to speak your mind with me, and to count on you being able to handle it if I speak mine. I respect you enough to believe you don't need me to be a pretender around you. You can have your beliefs and preferences, I can have mine, and we can both be open about them. We can even disagree openly, without having to act as if we agreed on everything."

There's a stronger virtue yet: *Love.* Love says, "Even though I disagree with you, and even if I don't like everything about you, I'm still going to treat you as a friend, the best I possibly can."

Tips for Talking with Your Teen

Sometimes the best answer is a question. I've got a few questions to suggest for you:

What do you mean by tolerance?

What do you mean by intolerance?

Is intolerance the same as disagreeing with another person's values or views?

So if you're telling me my values or views are wrong, aren't you being just as intolerant as you say I'm being?

You see, people get confused over what tolerance means, and they forget that the way they're calling other people intolerant can be intolerant in itself.

Those aren't the only questions you could ask. If you have time to talk—time enough to really explain what you mean—you might be able to help them think it through better than they ever have before by asking, "Why is it important to be tolerant? Have you ever considered that mutual respect might be even better?"

That's going to be a new thought to most of your friends, so they probably won't have a clue what you're talking about. Here's how you could explain it:

Suppose, for example, I tell you I don't think gay sex is okay, and you say you disagree with me. Suppose we could really talk about it honestly. Behind it all, we'd also be telling each other we're okay with being real with each other. We'd be saying, too, that we respect each other enough to believe we can both handle it without losing our cool.

Your friends may not get it the first time. It's probably going to take a while. But if they can get a grip on how their demand for "tolerance" is intolerant itself, and if they can start to grab hold of the idea of mutual respect, you're making progress.

They could still come back and tell you that if you think gay sex isn't okay, then you're not respecting gay people. Stick with your convictions, okay? Tell them you respect them enough to be real with them and to believe they can handle people who are different from them.

"How can you think your morality is better than others', or that you're better than other people?"

The Challenge

"You Christians act like you're superior to everyone else. What makes you think your morality is so superior that you can impose it on us all?"

Truths Your Teen Needs to Know

Smug religionism ("I'm better than you are because I'm religious or godly") happens way too often, and when it does, it's not Christlike. Jesus was crucified by smug religionists. What others call "Christians' morality" isn't really ours anyway; it's God's revealed morality for everyone.

Digging Deeper

Jesus hates hypocrisy. Nothing drew so much of his criticism, or brought him into so much conflict, as the Pharisees and their self-satisfied hypocrisy. I call it "smug religionism." It's sin, and if we're guilty of it we need to face it as such, confess it, and make things right with those whom we've wronged.

Sometimes, though, when people accuse Christians of thinking our morality is better than everyone else's, it's because they misunderstand where morality comes from. (This will take a moment to explain, but it's important.) For most people today, "my morality" really means "*my* morality," meaning, *It's my own product. I've custom-made it for myself. It fits me well; after all, I'm the one who put it together.* It's like picking items off a cafeteria line. Each person looks over all the different moral options, selects the ones that seem to fit him or her, and packages them all together into his or her own morality.

Now, if that were a true picture of Christians' morality, our moral codes wouldn't be better than anyone else's, and it really would be wrong for us to push our views on others. God's morality isn't that way, though. Properly speaking, Christians don't think *our* morality is better than anyone else's. We believe *God's* moral standards are best for everyone. They're good for everyone because they come from the character of God himself. They matter for everyone because God is everyone's God and creator, and because he intends for every person to take him and his standards very seriously.

Does anyone follow God's ways perfectly? No. No one even comes close. We all have our failures, mistakes, blunders, and yes, sins. Smug religionists hide behind a facade of holiness. Genuine Christians are open about their need for grace. We're no better than anyone else—but the God we follow certainly is!

Tips for Talking with Your Teen

You might say something like this to your teen, always bearing in mind that this isn't a script; it's a guide for discussion:

When someone asks me what makes me think my morality is better than anyone else's, I have an easy answer. I don't! And if someone asks why I want to impose my morality on them, I have the same answer: I don't want to do that at all.

There's a nice element of surprise in that answer. It's bound to get them to ask other questions, like, "Hey, I thought that was what Christians did." That's when I say—and it's when you could say—"It isn't my morality; it's God's. I have to submit to it just as much as anyone else. And wouldn't you agree, if there's anyone who could set one moral standard that's right for everyone, it would be God? That's who I think we're dealing with here. I'm just glad his morality is a good kind of morality."

That's barely enough to get you started, though. You see, most people your age think morality and beliefs are for people to pick and choose according to what makes the most sense to them, or what they think fits them best. When they hear Christians saying there's a moral standard we know of that's right for everyone, they're likely to hear it as something else: that we've got a moral standard that's based on our religious preference, that it fits us, and that we think our preferred morality has to fit everyone else, too. That's not true; our morality doesn't come out of our preferences but from God himself. Most people aren't used to that concept, though.

So this may not be something you'll be able to explain real quickly. I think with most people you're going to have to take time talking and listening to them about where they think morality comes from. You'll need to do your own study, too, and you could start in on it by reading chapters 3 and 4 in Critical Conversations.

Here's what helps me the most, though. If I'm looking for a morality that fits, and if there's a God who designed me and really, really loves me—just like he loves everyone—how hard is it to agree that he designed morality in a way that fits us all?

"Anti-this, anti-that: you're just anti-gay!"

The Challenge

"You Christians are against sex, against choice, against equality—you just like to be *against* things. Your beef with homosexuality is just more of the same. You're anti-gay because being 'anti-' is what Christianity does best."

Truths Your Teen Needs to Know

It's true: Christianity does stand against a lot of things. But Christianity is still a positive answer, not a negative one. Every good thing has a bad thing opposite to it, so we can't avoid standing against some negatives while we're standing for positives.

Digging Deeper

It's a shame we Christians have let our reputation be defined by what we're against. We've made it clear we're *against* extramarital sex and anything related to homosexuality; we haven't made it as clear that we're *for* healthy marriages, healthy families, disease-free living, and the maximized intimacy that comes from a fully trusting marital relationship. Maybe it's just been easier all along to say, "Hey, don't do that!"[2]

So we have some corrective work to do. The place to start is with ourselves: are we completely convinced that whatever God is against, it's because he is for some positive, good thing on the opposite side of it?

God is good, and his commands are for our good. Earlier (chapters 3 and 4) we saw that there are good—I mean really *good*—reasons for sex to be kept within the boundaries of natural marriage between

---

2. Legalism has always seemed attractive, even though it's wrong. See my article: Tom Gilson, "The Map or the Fuel? Living by Grace," Thinking Christian blog, June 2, 2009, www.thinkingchristian.net/posts/2009-06/the-map-or-the-fuel -living-by-grace/.

a man and a woman.[3] In other words, there's a positive side to our stand against homosexuality (and all other extramarital sex). Its purpose is to support and help preserve marriage for the sake of couples' genuine growth and fulfillment, for the nurturing and growth of the next generation, and for the greater health of all society. It's also for our spiritual growth, because a life focused on sensuality isn't a life that's focused on spiritual development.

I'd like to take this one step further, with a point that applies to many more situations than the one we're looking at here. I've had several great conversations starting out with, "Tell me some ways you've run into this Christian negativity. I wonder what that's been like for you." I suggest you try that sometime. Listen to the other person's answer. Make it clear that you care about them, and about what they're telling you.

That can open the door for further questions like these:

- Is it possible that Christianity isn't as anti-everything as you've been led to believe?
- Specifically, what leads you to think Christianity is opposed to sex?
- Do you think we're opposed to all sex?
- Have you ever considered the possibility that there could be a good side to the warnings and boundaries the Bible sets?
- Can you think of anything good that could come out of a person being willing to say no to temptations?

Any one of these questions could open up a long discussion, which is good. Some conversations really do take time.

Tips for Talking with Your Teen

When someone says, "You're just anti-gay, just like you're anti-everything else," you can count on having a long talk about it. You'll

---

3. I'll approach the same issue again from another angle later in part 3 when I discuss the topic, "Same-sex marriage takes nothing away from traditional marriage."

need to explain at least two things to your teen before they can explain it in turn to someone else. The first is that Christians believe that being *against* homosexuality is being *for* something else. The second is *why* we believe that's true.

You might say something like this to your teen, always bearing in mind that this isn't a script; it's a guide for discussion:

Unfortunately, most people today have never heard that being against homosexuality is being for something else, something good. Try telling someone that, and there's a good chance they'll look at you like you've just floated in from outer space. That's actually a prime time to ask the other person simply to treat you as a fellow human being.

You could say, "I know you think I'm crazy, but I'd like you at least to see that I'm a human being just like you. I'm not a monster or a space alien, I have human feelings, and I care about people, too. Can you imagine that as a possibility?"

Some people won't go even that far with you. There may be nothing more you can do with them except agree to disagree. Most people will go at least that distance, though. The next question you ask them could be, "Do you think it's possible that someone like me might have thought through some actual reasons not to accept homosexuality (or gay marriage)?"

Do you see how slowly I'm recommending you take this? Sure, you could jump straight into a list of reasons for what you believe, but that approach has a lot going against it. It sets up the conversation as "me against you." The person you're talking with is likely to rev up his anti-Christian prejudices to full speed. There's no getting through to anyone that way.

It's better to take it in small steps. Suppose you only get as far as helping someone see that—just maybe!—Christianity might not be an uncaring, unthinking, intolerant religion after all. That might not sound like much progress, but it's better than where they were when you started!

You might even be able to move beyond that. The person you're talking with might open herself up to the possibility that we Christians have reasons for our position. That's better yet! You've begun helping her see that her impression of Christianity might not be true, and that there could be good, positive reasons to say no to some things. The door is open to keep the discussion going. That's excellent!

Don't be surprised, though, if people find it hard to go there with you right away. It takes time, prayer, and the work of God for a person to be able to see and accept God's total and perfect goodness.

Remember that logic alone will never argue anyone out of negative impressions—especially when there's some truth to those impressions, as there is in this case. We really are anti-homosexuality, after all.

So set your expectations accordingly, and don't feel like you need to score a quick win. If you can open the door to genuine friendship (or keep an already existing friendship from falling apart), that's enough of a win right there: you're demonstrating through actions that you aren't against LGBT people (or their supporters) as people.

"Why won't you just let us be?"

The Challenge

"You Christians keep meddling in other people's business. Why won't you just let us be?"

Truths Your Teen Needs to Know

Christians didn't start the fight over gay rights. We're the defenders, not the aggressors.

Digging Deeper

This question has echoes in a similar one that Christians sometimes ask, too: "Why do we have to be so involved in these nasty culture wars?" It's as if we were the ones who started the controversies and made them political—as if we've been the aggressors, in other words. We haven't been. We still aren't. We're defenders.

Same-sex marriage was a revolutionary idea that came on the scene by way of a carefully crafted campaign to "overhaul" the rest of us (see chapter 2). It was an insurgency, an invasion upon long-established moral values. The Supreme Court may have legalized gay marriage, but that can't change the fact that we're still defending truths that have been established for centuries.

I'm not saying that being on the defensive side makes us right. I'm saying instead that the question, "Why won't you just let us be?" is misdirected. Consider this example. Suppose some large corporate retail store were trying to muscle in on all the small businesses in your small town, and the local merchants organized an effort to keep the store out (before it was built) and to keep their customers loyal like before (after the new store was built). Would it make sense for the corporation to complain, "Why won't you just leave us alone?" Obviously not. That would just display confusion over who's doing what to whom.

This plea to "let us just get along" is weak for another reason, too: it's another way of asking, "Why don't you just give up and let us have our way?" Seen in that light, it seems pretty self-centered, doesn't it?

Tips for Talking with Your Teen

You'll likely need to share some of the points in "Digging Deeper" when you talk with your teen about this. Just read it together and have a conversation about it. Then you might say something like this to your teen, always bearing in mind that this isn't a script; it's a guide for discussion:

I know you don't like to argue with your friends. I don't blame you. Actually this is a good time not to argue, because arguing itself might just prove their point. The best, first way to answer, "Why won't you just let us be?" is by getting along, though of course without compromising what you believe.

Still, you'll want to explain things to your friends. You might want to tell the story of the corporation moving in on the small town [see above], and then ask, "Does this help you understand what it's like from my side? It's about who's doing what to whom. We're not so much the aggressors here after all, are we?"

Then—if you're really ready for it—look the other person in the eye and say, "I take this position because of my principles. Are you asking me to give up my principles so you can have your way?"

"If you're homophobic, maybe you're a closet gay or lesbian yourself."

The Challenge

"If you're afraid of homosexuality or you hate LGBT causes, could it be because you're afraid of your own same-sex impulses?"

Truths Your Teen Needs to Know

This charge may fit a few people—*very* few. For the most part, though, it's an irresponsible overuse of pop psychology. Not only that, but it contradicts what LGBT people typically say about their own sexual preferences.

Digging Deeper

For the great majority of people who are asked this question, the answer is simple: No. That ought to settle it.

Some challengers might come back and ask, "Are you *sure* you haven't repressed those feelings?" Face it: that comes from too much pop psychology. The answer is still simple: "Yes, I'm sure." That really should be all it takes.

The odd thing about this challenge is that LGBT people typically tell us they would find it impossible to feel (or to live) any other way—yet this challenge implies that it's possible for us to suppress *our* same-sex attractions. If they can't suppress their same-sex attractions, why do they think others can?

Tips for Talking with Your Teen

You might say something like this to your teen, always bearing in mind that this isn't a script; it's a guide for discussion:

The simple answer to this question is no. A respectful person would accept that. You don't need to prove yourself. Actually, to try to prove yourself would be a trap, especially if they're the type who comes back at you and says, "See, there you go again, proving you can't admit it!" They're being rude, that's all.

If they press you on it, don't defend; instead, turn the question around: "LGBT people say they can't help but be the way they are, right? But here you are telling me I'm LGBT on the inside, but I'm covering it up so well, not even I know about it. How does that make sense?"

This isn't about catching them in some kind of "gotcha." It's about taking the focus off their rude accusations against you. It also helps show them that their pop psychology doesn't make sense in the first place.

By the way, I advise you just to ignore the parts about you being afraid or hateful when they try this challenge on you.

"Hate is not a family value."

The Challenge
"You claim to support family values. Hate isn't one of them."

Truths Your Teen Needs to Know
Every word in that slogan is true, but this common bumper-sticker saying has nothing to do with our opposition to LGBT activism.

Digging Deeper
For this slogan to mean anything, opposing the LGBT agenda would have to be equal to hating LGBT people. It's possible, though, to stand for natural marriage and healthy sexual morality, and do it without hating. (We've discussed that often enough throughout this book.) People oppose all kinds of things—decisions, laws, advice, guidance, rules, and opinions—without hating the people involved.

Rarely will any of us need to answer this question in conversation with another person. It's a bumper sticker, not something that people actually say to each other. When I see it I just smile and say to myself, "Those are nothing but empty words." You could say the same thing to your teen, if you're driving together and see that bumper sticker in front of you. Consider it a good teaching moment, an opportunity to explain just why it's empty.

If the unlikely happens, and someone does mention this to you or your teen in conversation, you might follow the guidance I gave in the topic, "You're a hater" (pp. 98–100). Otherwise there's no need for us even to go into "Tips for Talking with Your Teen" for this topic.

"You're harming LGBT people with your intolerance."

The Challenge

"Your intolerance is causing LGBT persons a high rate of depression, and anxiety, and even suicide."

Truths Your Teen Needs to Know

LGBT individuals display a higher than average rate of depression, anxiety, and suicidal thoughts and behaviors. This is often blamed on other people's intolerance. There are so many potential contributing factors, however, that it's simplistic to pin so much LGBT distress on just one cause. Christians do need to distinguish between actually harmful behaviors on the one hand, and truth-telling that does no harm (even though it may hurt) on the other hand.

Digging Deeper

LGBT people tend to experience a higher level of stress, anxiety, and depression than heterosexuals.[4] A disproportionately large number attempt suicide; tragically, many of them succeed.[5] One common

---

4. See for example, from the British National Health Service, "Mental Health Issues if You're Gay, Lesbian, or Bisexual," last reviewed July 17, 2014, www.nhs.uk /Livewell/LGBhealth/Pages/Mentalhealth.aspx; Joseph G. Kosciw, Emily A. Greytak, Neal A. Palmer, and Madelyn J. Boesen, "The 2013 National School Climate Survey: The Experiences of Lesbian, Gay, Bisexual and Transgender Youth in Our Nation's Schools," New York: Gay, Lesbian & Straight Education Network, 2014), www.glsen.org/sites/default/files/2013%20National%20School%20Climate%20 Survey%20Full%20Report_0.pdf; and "Lesbian, Gay, Bisexual and Transgender Health," Centers for Disease Control and Prevention, last updated November 12, 2014, www.cdc.gov/lgbthealth/youth.htm.

5. See the brief fact sheet at American Association of Suicidology, "Suicidal Behavior Among LGBT Youth," 2014, accessed July 9, 2015, suicidology.org/Portals /14/docs/Resources/FactSheets/2011/LGBT2014.pdf; or the technical article, M. E. Eisenberg and M. D. Resnick, "Suicidality Among Gay, Lesbian and Bisexual Youth: The Role of Protective Factors," *J Adolesc Health* 39, no. 5 (2006). The Eisenberg and Resnick study suggests that the chief contributors to suicidal thoughts among LGB youth are a lack of (a) family connectedness, (b) adult caring, and

explanation for this is that they're hurting from the stigma, shame, and embarrassment that have been wrongly placed on them by society. If everyone would just accept that their sexuality or gender identity is good and right and proper, they could find relief from some of the stress and anxiety.

This is a serious charge. If Christians are guilty of harming others this way, we should repent immediately. That's a big *if*, though, and in fact the charge is seriously oversimplified at best, if not totally false. The charge implies that Christian intolerance is the one big source of LGBT distress. The reality is that while LGBT people do experience real intolerance, a lot of it surely comes from non-Christians and nonreligious people, and intolerance isn't likely to be the sole source of their distress anyway. Let's take a more thoughtful, less simplistic look at the possible causes, some of which might be:

1. Being shunned, teased, bullied, assaulted—all the ways malicious people sometimes oppress other people.
2. Experiencing rejection at home.
3. Facing discrimination in housing, employment, etc.
4. Being a minority culture whose story isn't validated or appreciated by the majority (which used to be the case, but certainly isn't any longer!).
5. Being told that their desires and actions are morally wrong.
6. Being prevented (until now) from having their relationships validated as marriages.
7. Simply being LGBT, that is, there might be some degree of relational/emotional distress that is unavoidably associated with the LGBT orientation and/or experience.

How much does each of these contribute to LGBT distress? The story we hear from LGBT activists is that the first six factors account for pretty much all their problems, while the seventh one, being

---

(c) school safety defined simply in terms of whether the student feels safe at school, going there, and coming home.

LGBT, is neutral or possibly even a positive contributor to mental health. This should be open to question.

First, not all that feels bad is harmful. I'll return to that in a moment. Second, it's unclear from the research that being LGBT is intrinsically neutral or positive and that LGBT persons would get along fine if only it weren't for all the other stuff they have to deal with. As I wrote in chapter 2, the mental health professions made a non-evidence-based decision over forty years ago to declassify homosexuality as a mental disorder. Since then researchers have shown little interest in confirming the accuracy of that assessment. Studies have gone both ways, and research on both sides of the issue has often been clouded over with bias. Some of those charges are true. (See for example the discussion in chapter 6 on potential bias in LGBT suicide-rate research.)

There are objective signs, though, indicating that there's more to LGBT distress than others' intolerance. Gay men report having an extremely high number of lifetime sexual partners, strongly suggesting there's some need in them they can't seem to satisfy successfully.[6] Domestic violence is considerably higher among same-sex couples than opposite-sex couples (married or cohabiting), according to research reported on a pro-LGBT website.[7] The same study

---

6. Brown, *Can You Be Gay and Christian?* Kindle loc. 3399; also, Gus Cairns, "Consistent Decline in Partner Numbers in US Gay Men in Last Decade, But No Change in Condom Use," NAM AidsMap, April 25, 2013, www.aidsmap .com/Consistent-decline-in-partner-numbers-in-US-gay-men-in-last-decade -but-no-change-in-condom-use/page/2635086/.

A gay man in Amsterdam, where anti-LGBT attitudes are uncommon, told a researcher, "Amsterdam is like a big pond of fish. One day you catch a beautiful fish and it looks good and it tastes good. But instead of keeping it and being happy with this beautiful species, you just throw it back because you don't know what bigger fish you could catch the next day. There are too many fish out there in the pond." In Roger Peabody, "'Not Quite Normal'—Exploring Poor Mental Health in Gay Men," February 6, 2014, www.aidsmap.com/Not-quite-normal-exploring -poor-mental-health-in-gay-men/page/2824071/.

7. J. D. Glass, "2 Studies That Prove Domestic Violence Is an LGBT Issue," *Advocate*, September 4, 2014, www.advocate.com/crime/2014/09/04/2-studies-prove -domestic-violence-lgbt-issue. On gay couples' relational issues, see Jason

found that three times as many gay men (21.5%) had experienced domestic violence at some point in their lives as straight men (7.1%). Among women the comparison was 35.4% of lesbians versus 20.4% of straight women.

Some portion of these reported difficulties is undoubtedly due to anti-LGBT stigma, but it's doubtful that all of it can be blamed on just one thing. There are many other factors that could contribute, remember. Still we have a responsibility to consider how Christians might be causing harm to LGBT persons, and we have to take seriously the fact that some of us really have been guilty of shunning, teasing, bullying, even assaulting gays, lesbians, and transgender persons. That's wrong. We need to put an immediate halt—as far as it's in our power to do so—to all such oppression.

Meanwhile many of us are speaking out to say that homosexual practice is morally wrong. Undoubtedly this causes distress among LGBT persons. Being criticized never feels good. We continue anyway, knowing that we're causing them pain. Why would we do this, and shouldn't we stop this, too? If we're speaking out maliciously, then yes, definitely we should stop. If we're speaking the truth in love, though, the answer is that we have an obligation to continue despite the pain we might be causing.

Feelings are great for some purposes, but not so much for others. I really love donuts. I like to brag, "I'm strong. I can resist the donut temptation—just as long as nobody offers me one, I don't see one, and I don't drive by a store that sells them." Donuts make me feel good, but they aren't the healthiest things I could eat. When it comes to discerning what donuts really do for me, my feelings don't match reality.

Feelings are often deceptive that way. God's Word, on the other hand, is a completely reliable guide to what's true. The Scriptures take a much longer and deeper view of reality than our emotions can,

---

Richwine, "Will Gay Couples Divorce More Than Straight Ones? (And Will We Even Be Allowed to Study It?)" National Review, *The Corner*, July 7, 2014, www .nationalreview.com/corner/382154/will-gay-couples-divorce-more-straight -ones-and-will-we-even-be-allowed-study-it-jason.

though without overlooking that we have emotions, and emotions matter.

There's a saying in the business world: "Reality is your friend." You can make your world seem okay by refusing to acknowledge facts you don't like, but in the end, reality always catches up with you. Not only that, but reality has a way of making us adjust to it, rather than adjusting itself to us. The sooner we start adjusting ourselves to reality, the better.

God is the deepest reality, and indeed, *God is our friend* if we join our hearts to his through faith in Christ. His moral codes are real, and so is his goodness. Therefore to tell the truth about homosexuality—gently, understandingly, yet consistently—is to point people toward God's real goodness and his moral character. The news may not be pleasant to all ears, but for deep eternal reasons, it's good.

Admittedly we don't always speak it the best way, and sometimes we cause needless pain and offense. That's our failing, not the Bible's. Truth is real, and truth is good. If we speak it in love, wisdom, and grace (Eph. 4:15; Col. 4:6), we're doing good, not harm, no matter what others may say.

We're doing a good thing when we speak the truth in love, but we must never forget we're doing it in a painful way. My own heart test as I share the truth is, *What am I feeling inside: gleeful victory or empathetic grief?* As a parent you know that delivering discipline can be as painful to you as it is to your child. It's good if we feel that pain; it keeps us from losing touch with the humanness of the person we're sharing with. It keeps us from losing touch with God's own grief over the damage sin causes.

There's a huge difference between speaking truth to win arguments and speaking truth to persuade others in love.

Tips for Talking with Your Teen

You might say something like this to your teen, always bearing in mind that this isn't a script; it's a guide for discussion:

LGBT people and their supporters have a vested interest in making us feel guilty for criticizing them. It packs a powerful punch when they tie LGBT suicides to our criticisms. They seem to forget that there are many other things that could also contribute to the distress they feel. That's the key to your answer to this charge. If someone tells you Christians' intolerance is causing LGBT young people to consider suicide, you can ask, "Do you think that's the only thing going on in gays' or lesbians' lives that's bothering them?" As you think it through together you should be able to come up with a list like the seven causes in the "Digging Deeper" section here. Then ask, "Don't you think it's possible that some of these other things might be partly to blame, too?"

As you do this, make it clear that you're against bullying, teasing, shunning, and any other action of that sort. Help them see that disagreeing with someone's moral choices isn't necessarily any of those things. Reality is what reality is, after all, even if it's hard to face. You're convinced (I hope!) that same-sex physical intimacy does long-term spiritual harm. You know that's why Christians need to speak the truth, even though it may hurt in the short run. We need to warn people away from real harm in the long run.

Most LGBT supporters will have trouble accepting that, unfortunately. You could use the information in Critical Conversations to try to persuade them. It won't be easy, though, and you can't take responsibility for convincing them. If you can at least be satisfied in your own mind that it's okay for Christians to speak the truth in love, it will help you remain confident in your convictions without carrying a load of guilt. As your parent, I'm hoping you can at least get that far.

Meanwhile, I hope you'll let your heart break over the real pain that LGBT persons experience, no matter what or who is to blame. I hope you'll do everything you can to make sure that no one around you does anything that's genuinely harmful to LGBT people. I want you to be one of the most vocal anti-bullying people around. That's speaking the truth, too, after all.

GROUP B: REGARDING SOCIAL POLICY

The topics in group B of part 3 all have to do with social policy, including gay marriage. The Supreme Court rejected our opinion but that won't make the issues go away. We still have our principles; we still stand for what we stand for. The same moral challenges will keep coming our way, and they could be sharper than before since they'll be coming with the added punch, "Even the Supreme Court says you're wrong!"

So this section is about standing strong, holding on to our Christian beliefs, and being able to explain not only what's true but also what's good about them. It isn't about campaigning to keep marriage laws intact anymore. Instead it's about showing the truth and the goodness of God in Jesus Christ—which is what it should always be about anyway.

"You're on the wrong side of history."

The Challenge

"You're on the wrong side of history—gay rights is an idea whose time has come."

Truths Your Teen Needs to Know

The future isn't necessarily better than the past in every way. It isn't always what we expect, either. It makes no sense to try to consult tomorrow's opinions to discover what we ought to think today.

Digging Deeper

Does *later in time* necessarily mean *better*? In some ways, yes.

Science progresses, certainly, so we know more about nature, medicine, and such every year. Does that mean we know more about ethics every year, though? Do we know more about human relationships every year? Are today's poets and playwrights any more insightful than Shakespeare or Sophocles? Not likely! Even "scientific" progress sometimes turns out not to be what we expect. Here's an example you might not have known about: eugenics. Suppose it was 1911 right now, and you believed that scientific opinion always illuminated the way into the future. If so, you probably would have agreed with *Scientific American's* case for preventing "unfit" humans from "propagating." (Yes, this really appeared in *Scientific American* that year.)

> We know enough about the laws of heredity, we have enough statistics from insane asylums and prisons, we have enough genealogies, to show that, although we may not be able directly to improve the human race as we improve the breed of guinea pigs, rabbits or cows, because of the rebellious spirit of mankind, yet the time has come when the lawmaker should join hands with the scientist, and at least check the propagation of the unfit.[1]

This was during the day of the eugenics movement for the scientifically based improvement of humanity, through sterilizing and/or eliminating the "weaker specimens" among us. If you had believed in being on the "right side of history" then, you probably would have also agreed with what A. F. Tredgold, "medical expert" to the Royal Commission on the Feeble-Minded, had to say in a treatise he wrote about dealing with the insane, the feeble-minded, paupers, and criminals. He wrote,

---

1. "The Early Days of Eugenics: The Science of Breeding Better Men," *Scientific American*, May 25, 2011, www.scientificamerican.com/article/eugenics-the-early-days/.

At the same time it is clear that the presence of these degenerates constitutes a grave danger to civilization and to the future progress of man. What, then, must be done? I think the course is clear. Whilst extending to them our ready compassion, and whilst treating them with humane care, we must, in the interests of posterity, take such steps as will ensure that they do not propagate their kind. In other words we must apply the principle of selective breeding.

It is this which is the object of Eugenics; the science for which we are indebted to the late revered Sir Francis Galton. . . .

Progress in the future must be based upon the fundamental principles which have governed it in the past, namely, the selection of the fit and the rejection of the unfit.[2]

If you had opposed eugenics in 1911, people would have told you that you were against science and the forward march of progress. This was, tragically, the same march that led straight to Hitler's "life unworthy of living" and the eugenics-driven plan to rid the world of its so-called lesser races, especially Jews.

Where has history gone since then? What happened to eugenics? What happened to its "forward march of progress"?[3] It's marched right off the map. History has almost completely forgotten about it.

Now, undeniably progress does happen. Our society has advanced ethically in important ways, most obviously in our treatment of ethnic and national minorities. There *is* such a thing as getting better over time, but it isn't *time* that makes us better. Ethical advance comes by way of moving closer to a true ethical standard, not just by coming along later in history.

---

2. A. F. Tredgold, "Eugenics and the Future Progress of Man," *The Eugenics Review* 3, no. 2 (1911): 112–13, 117.

3. See further Thomas William O'Donnell, "The Strength and Vigor of the Race: California Labor Law and Race Preservation in the Progressive Era" (diss., California State University, Sacramento, 2009), 37.

Tips for Talking with Your Teen

So you might say something like this to your teen, always bearing in mind that this isn't a script; it's a guide for discussion:

I have some questions you could ask someone who says we're on the wrong side of history:

Is today always better than yesterday?

Do we really understand human nature better than the great artists, poets, and playwrights of Greece and Rome?

Are we supposed to judge our actions today based on what people fifty years from now will think of us? How are we supposed to know that already?

Did you know there was a time when the scientifically and socially 'progressive' view was that 'unfit' people should be sterilized? Did you know that this was in America and England, not Nazi Germany?

How much do we really know about public opinion fifty or a hundred years from now, anyway?

The point is this. Suppose gay rights really were a good idea: it wouldn't be because "history is going that way." We don't know where history is going, and where it goes isn't always progress anyway.

"Some day, Christians will be embarrassed over opposing gay rights, just like you're embarrassed over Christians who opposed civil rights."

The Challenge

"Christians in the middle of the twentieth century, including many preachers, stood against civil rights for African Americans. Look what an embarrassment that is to Christianity now. Christians in the future will be embarrassed over you just the same for opposing gay rights."

Truths Your Teen Needs to Know

This is a variation on the previous topic, "You're on the wrong side of history." It counts on future opinion to tell us what we should think today. It's true that many Christians, including Christian leaders, stood against civil rights in the twentieth century. Some of them even used the Bible to support their prejudices, a fact that undermines our witness still today. Not all of them did that, though, and regardless, the gay-rights situation is so different from previous civil-rights discussions, there's no good basis even for comparing them.

Digging Deeper

The language of "rights" is so central to America's culture and conscience, and it's been such a central topic in the same-sex marriage debate, it's going to take a bit of work to loosen the emotional knots around it and think rationally. The key issue for us to work on is, *what kind of rights did Blacks campaign for, and how similar are gay rights?* The facts make it clear: there's no comparison at all. The LGBT experience has been nothing like the African-American experience; gay rights are nothing like civil rights; and those who opposed civil rights ignored clear biblical teachings, whereas we who oppose gay rights are clearly following biblical instructions.

1. The LGBT experience has been nothing like the African-American experience.
African Americans have long suffered unjust disadvantages in employment, housing, and more. In most of these domains, LGBT people aren't being discriminated against; they're at parity with the rest of society. Therefore, if there is any civil rights dimension to the gay-rights cause at all, it's on a far lesser scale than it has been for African Americans.

I don't mean to say that LGBT people have never suffered unjust discrimination, and I certainly don't mean to imply that a little injustice is okay as long as it isn't a lot. I do want to point out that many African Americans object strenuously to claims that the LGBT Americans' struggle has been anything like theirs. Ernest Owens, a gay black man, wrote an impassioned plea in the Huffington Post, saying,

> So I say this with the utmost sincerity: please Gay America, stop comparing the current fight for LGBT rights to that of the civil rights movement. It is not only historically and culturally inaccurate, but personally offensive to the very gays of color you strive to also advocate for.[4]

Hip-hop record executive Adam Thomason lists five reasons "gay is not the new black":

1. You have never seen—and won't see—"heterosexual only" and "gay only" water fountains, diners, buses, schools, in light of 75 years of oppressive Jim Crow laws....
2. You have not—and won't—see homosexuals snatched away from their families at birth for the purpose of division and dehumanization....

---

4. Ernest Owen, "No, Gay Isn't the New Black," HuffPost Gay Voices, *The Blog*, July 8, 2014, www.huffingtonpost.com/ernest-owens/no-gay-isnt-the-new-black_b _5567150.html.

3. Homosexual men/women have never endured a slave trade for generations and witnessed their ancestors dying by the numbers during a "Middle Passage" and being sold for raw goods. . . .

4. Homosexuals have never been—or will be considered—noncitizens by laws of the United States that rob them of inalienable rights. . . .

5. Homosexuals will never face a societal norm that allows—and even promotes—them to be beaten because they are seen as property and treated like cattle with scripture as a basis for justification.[5]

Now, wherever LGBT people experience discrimination in employment, wages, housing, or any other domain of life where sexual orientation or private practices are irrelevant, all people of goodwill should want them to experience justice in the form of equal treatment under the law. Otherwise there's a world of difference between civil rights for racial minorities and marriage rights for gays.

2. Gay rights are nothing like civil rights.[6]

There was a time when African Americans were regarded as less than human, and therefore less than fully deserving of human rights. Somehow most of us have failed to see what really happened when African Americans gained new legal rights. Those rights did not come to them through creating any new rights on their behalf, but instead through the simple (although belated) recognition that they

5. Adam Thomason, "The People's District: 5 Reasons Gay Is Not the New Black," Forth District, January 29, 2014, forthdistrict.com/5-reasons-gay-is-not-the-new -black/.

6. This section is a condensed version of an article I wrote for *BreakPoint* in 2015: Tom Gilson, "Gay Rights vs. Civil Rights: Not Even Close," *BreakPoint*, July 15, 2015, www.breakpoint.org/features-columns/breakpoint-columns/entry/2 /27817. Some might object that minorities have requested special rights in the form of affirmative action, but that is more accurately seen as a privilege or entitlement granted minorities in certain defined circumstances to correct past injustices, not a right.

are fully human. Think about it: human rights for minorities were never about new rights being created for them. They have always been about ancient rights being newly applied to them.

Gay rights are different, especially gay marriage. Court decisions in favor of gay marriage have never granted anyone access to existing rights or to a historically existing institution; they've created new rights and a new institution instead.

Even the language tells the story: how often have you heard anyone cry out for "Black rights," the way so many have clamored "gay rights"? Blacks never campaigned for Black rights. They campaigned for *civil* rights, that is, ordinary *human* rights.

3. Those who opposed civil rights ignored clear biblical teachings, whereas we who oppose gay rights have clear biblical justification for doing so.

There are deep biblical principles supporting civil rights for minorities. All persons are fully human, created in God's image, and therefore deserve to be treated as fully human. Admittedly this moral principle has been tested and contested over time, and sometimes it seems like we've failed the test as often as we've passed it. Nevertheless it's clearly supported by the Bible, all the way back to the first chapter of Genesis.

In contrast to that, the moral principle behind the "right" to gay marriage—the idea that same-sex intimacy is worthy of celebrating, and that marriage need not be for opposite-sex couples after all—has been newly invented for our times.

From the founding of our country until recent days, Americans honored the view that human (civil) rights were endowed unto us by our Creator. The "right" to gay marriage, in contrast, was created in the past few years by a judicial system that has also (arguably, at least) invented for itself the right to invent new rights.

Again, human rights for minorities are firmly based in Scripture, beginning in our common humanness in the image of God in Genesis 1, while sexual intimacy for same-sex couples is clearly disallowed in Scripture. When Christians denied human rights to minorities, they were obviously wrong by the Bible's standards. When we dispute marriage rights for same-sex couples today, we have every reason to believe we're doing the right thing by scriptural standards.

In sum, that means that when activists try to invoke fear in us with the threat of some future generation of Christians being embarrassed by us the same way we're embarrassed by Christians who denied minorities their human rights, we can see that warning for what it is: a scare tactic. Civil rights for minorities are different from marriage rights for same-sex couples—so different, there isn't any good reason to think yesterday's lessons about civil rights have any application to today's questions about gay rights.

Tips for Talking with Your Teen

This is a triple-barreled challenge. For one thing it implies that we're making a basic mistake by using the Bible to make our decisions, and for another it's connected to the charge that we're on the wrong side of history. Those aspects of the question are covered elsewhere: "You're just like the southerners who used the Bible to defend slavery," and of course, "You're on the wrong side of history." The third barrel is the one we're specifically concerned with here: the matter of civil rights and gay rights.

You might say something like this to your teen, always bearing in mind that this isn't a script; it's a guide for discussion:

The first thing you have to find out when you hear this challenge is what kind of rights the other person is talking about. If it's about LGBT people being discriminated against in jobs, housing, or other situations where sexuality and sexual behavior don't matter, then feel free to agree! LGBT people deserve basic human rights just like all humans do.

Lately, though, this challenge has most often been about marriage. In that case, it's helpful to ask a few questions to clarify what they're talking about. For example, you could ask them to explain what it is that makes gay marriage a right; and then keep the conversation going by asking, "What is it that makes anything a right? Where do rights come from? How do we know what's really a right and what isn't?" Chances are the person you're talking with won't have much of an answer. *If you don't start with God as America's founders did, these questions are very difficult.*

That's just an introduction to help them recognize this isn't the easy, obvious issue they probably thought it was. Once they've discovered that, you're ready to ask the questions that really count:

> When basic civil rights were extended to racial minorities, did Americans have to invent any new rights for them? What about gay rights? Do you see the difference?

> Figuring out what makes something a right is hard, isn't it? So how do you know gay marriage should be counted as a new right?

> If you don't know that, then is it fair to haul out the big-gun, emotionally charged language of 'civil rights' when we're talking about this? Aren't you skipping a step?

> The Supreme Court has declared gay marriage to be a new right. That makes it so in a legal sense, but does it guarantee that the court was morally correct? Remember: it was wrong on civil rights with the Dred Scott decision in 1857 (denying human rights to enslaved humans).

Don't count on this being an easy win. People are so used to thinking of gay marriage as a civil right, they won't give up that thought just because you've shown them they jumped the gun getting there. You'll know it, though, and if nothing else, you can let that knowledge keep you strong on the inside when people push you on the outside.

"You're a bigot."

The Challenge
"You're a bigot and you're prejudiced against LGBT people."

Truths Your Teen Needs to Know
This is a powerful accusation, but a closer look at the definition of *bigot* reveals that it doesn't necessarily apply to people who disagree with the advance of gay rights.

Digging Deeper
I've been writing about gay rights (among many other things) at ThinkingChristian.net, Breakpoint.org and other websites for years. I can't tell you how many times I've been told online that I'm a bigot. In face-to-face conversation, it seems that people are less likely to deliver such a strong insult, though it did happen to me once in a shouting match (of sorts) with a student on a college campus. I was talking; he was shouting. He shouted a lot, actually, repeatedly criticizing me and other Christians for our bigotry in denying gays their rights. I kept trying to answer calmly; he kept cutting me off. At last I was able to get a full question in, and it was about rights, too: "Does a Christian have the right to finish a sentence?" He shot back, "No!"

That was an unusual encounter. The great majority of my face-to-face conversations with gays and gay-rights advocates (unlike online encounters) have been far more normal and pleasant. So my guess is, neither you nor your teen may ever be called a bigot to your face.

That doesn't mean you won't hear the bigot charge being sent your way indirectly. It's everywhere: on the Internet, in the media, in conversations overheard in the football stands, in fact almost anywhere we go. We need to know how to answer this challenge wherever we run into it—even if it's just in the privacy of our own consciences.

Merriam-Webster's online dictionary defines *bigot* as:

: a person who strongly and unfairly dislikes other people, ideas, etc. : a bigoted person; *especially* : a person who hates or refuses to accept the members of a particular group (such as a racial or religious group)

: a person who is obstinately or intolerantly devoted to his or her own opinions and prejudices; *especially* : one who regards or treats the members of a group (as a racial or ethnic group) with hatred and intolerance[7]

It's a good definition, but it has some flaws. One place it goes wrong is in lumping "other people" together with "ideas," as if there were no big difference between strongly disliking some people and strongly disliking some ideas. In fact, that's exactly where much of the confusion on this issue stems from: the idea that disliking LGBT-related ideas (values, principles, etc.) is the same as disliking LGBT persons. It isn't. The two "dislikes" are distinctly different.

Still, this definition gives us a lot to work with. Let's take it a piece at a time and see how well it fits. I'll use myself as a test case.

- *I'm a bigot if I strongly and unfairly dislike other people.* I can't think of any individual—much less an entire group of people —whom I "strongly dislike."
- *I'm a bigot if I strongly and unfairly dislike certain ideas.* I do dislike gay activism–related ideas, but I don't think my dislike is unfair, and I can give reasons to explain why. As we saw in the topic on intolerance, nobody can accept, agree with, or even like everyone's ideas, so does that mean *everyone* is a bigot? Hardly.
- *I'm a bigot if I hate members of another group for being a part of that group.* Honestly, I don't, so I'm not a bigot on that count.
- *I'm a bigot if I refuse to accept members of another group.* Here's another weak point in this definition. It's too loosely stated. What does *accept* mean? Does it mean being willing to have

---

7. *Merriam-Webster*, s.v., "bigot," accessed November 23, 2015, wwww.merriam -webster.com/dictionary/bigot.

them as friends? I'm not a bigot on that count. Does it mean accepting them into your group? That couldn't be a universal standard. The American College of Surgeons doesn't accept me into their group, and it certainly isn't because they're bigoted toward me! There are places were I should rightfully be accepted and others where I shouldn't.

So I don't know exactly what "refuse to accept" means here. I do know that if I'm in a group where a gay person has a rightful place—which depends on the group and the person, just as it does for any other group's membership decisions—then I'll accept that gay person. I'm not a bigot on that count.

- *I'm a bigot if I'm obstinately or intolerantly devoted to my own opinions or prejudices.* This part of the definition needs a longer look. It makes sense as long as we're clear on what *obstinately* means. (Once again, *intolerant* is an almost useless term, as explained in our earlier discussion of intolerance.) To be obstinate about holding on to my own opinions means I won't listen seriously to anything I don't already agree with. That's likely to be a form of bigotry. But in fact I'm not opposed to listening to others' views, evaluating them, and accepting what's good in them. So I don't see how I could be considered a bigot on that count.

What if I decide someone else's opinion is false, though? Does that make me a bigot? No, not in itself. Even if the other person was right about it and I was wrong, my disagreement wouldn't necessarily make me a bigot. No one who got the date of the French Revolution wrong on a history test was automatically a bigot for making that mistake. It's only bigotry if the error comes by way of an obstinate devotion to one's own view; but again, the key word is *obstinate.*

(Have you kept up with me so far? I might seem to be over-analyzing there. If so, take heart: it gets simpler again now.)

When it comes to the gay-rights controversy, there's no doubt that just about everyone on both sides of the issue is devoted to their views. So how do we decide who's being obstinate and who isn't? That's a hard question to get right, but it's amazingly easy to get wrong, and this is one way to do that: bypass all calm, reasoned conversation, and jump straight to the insult: "You're a bigot!"

Far too often, that's exactly what happens: Christians and other conservatives get labeled as bigots just because we disagree. Couldn't we just explain why we believe what we believe, before they slap a label like that on us?

- Finally, *I'm a bigot if I treat the members of some group with hatred or intolerance.* I've been accused of hatred and intolerance, to be sure, but as I've explained in previous topics in this book, those accusations are misdirected.

So am I a bigot? Not by Merriam-Webster's definition.

Are you a bigot? You'll have to examine yourself and decide. Just don't buy the prejudiced (and arguably bigoted) line that if you refuse to celebrate everything LGBT, that makes you a bigot. In fact, as I wrote under the topic "You're a hater," when others label you that way they're probably stereotyping. And while bigotry and stereotyping don't necessarily live in the same apartment, they're at least next-door neighbors.

Tips for Talking with Your Teen

You might say something like this to your teen, always bearing in mind that this isn't a script; it's a guide for discussion:

Is someone calling you a bigot? That's a strong accusation, so it makes me wonder, how angry are they? If they're saying it with a raised voice or clenched fists, just walk away and pray for a better time to talk later on.

If they're saying it in a friendlier manner—though it's hard to imagine how that could be—you should probably ask them calmly what they mean by it. You'll be surprised how many people use the word without knowing what it really means.

From there you should be prepared for the conversation to go either one way or another. The more common direction (since they're already insulting you) is for people to tell you that you're automatically a bigot—no matter what else might be true about you—if you don't agree with gay rights. That's actually a bigoted thing for them to say, since it's complete stereotyping, but don't expect to win them over by telling them that. It's better if you can either change the subject (maybe to one of the other topics in this book) or else walk away, rather than try to win a game of "Who's the real bigot here?"

　　If you're lucky, the conversation might go better than that. The person might actually try to explain why they think you're bigoted. If they do, you're probably going to find them talking about one of the other chal-lenges covered in Critical Conversations, *and you can forget about the bigotry charge and simply talk about whichever subject comes up.*

"You're against equality."

The Challenge

"This is all about marriage equality. Allowing gays to marry is a matter of equal treatment under the law, and if you oppose it, you're against the values that made our nation great, going all the way back to the Declaration of Independence."

Truths Your Teen Needs to Know

Everyone is in favor of marriage equality, believe it or not—and everyone (in a different sense) is opposed to marriage equality. No one *really* believes all relationships should be treated equally under the name of "marriage." Therefore "marriage equality" is a rhetorical shortcut that bypasses clear thinking.

Digging Deeper

"Marriage equality" was the gay marriage movement's central slogan leading up to the Supreme Court decision in June 2015. It was a savvy choice of words for their side. Equality is at the heart of all Western civilization, its importance deeply underscored everywhere from the civil rights battles in the United States to the ending of apartheid in South Africa. It's much more than a principle of government; it's a matter of doing what's right.

The problem is, even though it's a good and powerful term, it's never really been the right one to bring to the table for these discussions. No one really believes equality is what determines whether marriage policy is just or unjust. If it were, then marriage should really be equal for all: a sister marrying a brother, a parent marrying an adult child, a man marrying a woman who is already married to another man, foursomes marrying, and on and on.

That would be absurd, wouldn't it? No one thinks it makes sense to make *every* conceivable form of "marital" relationship equal. Everyone knows there have to be some limits. The question is, where are those limits? And that's the only question that counts. Everyone can say yes to the question, "Do you believe in marriage equality?"

The only thing people disagree on is where equality bumps into proper limits.

It's really that simple—except it's never easy to help people see the wrongheadedness of their favorite campaign slogan. There's a good example of how to explain it in the dialogue, "Phil and Alex on 'Marriage Equality,'" on my Thinking Christian blog.[8]

Tips for Talking with Your Teen

You might say something like this to your teen, always bearing in mind that this isn't a script; it's a guide for discussion:

Everyone agrees with marriage equality up to a point. The only question is where equality should end. The best way to help your friends see that is probably to ask them whether they think marriage equality reaches as far as married threesomes, fathers and sons marrying each other, or any other outrageous form of "marriage" you can count on them disagreeing with. Then ask them why those unions shouldn't be called "marriages."

Don't worry at this point whether their reasons are right or wrong, good or bad. Just point out that their reasons have nothing to do with equality: "See, you have principles you go by to decide what should count as marriage and what shouldn't, and your principles aren't based on equality. You don't believe in equality-plain-and-simple, you believe in equality-up-to-a-limit. So do I! We both believe in marriage equality. We both believe in limits to equality. We only disagree on where those limits belong. We can talk about that limit line all day long, but please don't forget that's what we're talking about—not about equality."

On one level this is really quite straightforward—yet it can be terribly difficult to succeed with in conversation. Equality is such a powerful word, same-sex marriage advocates don't like letting go of it. Don't be surprised, then, if you get some pushback, for example, "Your problem is that you don't believe in marriage equality for gays."

8. Tom Gilson, "Phil and Alex on 'Marriage Equality,'" November 29, 2012, Thinking Christian blog, www.thinkingchristian.net/posts/2012/11/phil-and-alex-on -marriage-equality.

Here's how you can simplify it. It's a variation on what I already suggested you say. Just start talking with them about where they draw the line. Listen to them carefully. Then ask them for the opportunity to explain why you draw the line where you do. Let that continue for a while, then you say, "Look at us: we've quit pretending our disagreements have to do with equality. We're disagreeing over where the line should be, where equality runs into a limit. Our disagreement has nothing to do with equality; it's all about the line where equality ends."

At that point, if the person understands what you're getting at, the whole "equality" challenge is disarmed, just as it should be. You'll have a lot left to talk about, because you've still got that disagreement over where the line should be. But at least, if the other person is listening rationally and reasonably, they will have come to realize the issue isn't marriage equality after all.

"Christians just want to discriminate against gays."

The Challenge
"Christians keep trying to discriminate against LGBT individuals."

Truths Your Teen Needs to Know
Not all discrimination is wrong; it depends on whether the reasons for it are just and proper.

Digging Deeper
May I begin by "discriminating" between *just* and *unjust* discrimination? To discriminate simply means to recognize a difference. It can be done either justly or unjustly. Discrimination by itself isn't necessarily bad. It becomes unjust only when it treats a difference that doesn't matter as if it did.

Consider race and employment, for example. Our country has been torn by on-the-job racial discrimination. It isn't just about skin color, by the way. I have a book of American folk songs, one of which (from the late nineteenth century) is titled, "No Irish Need Apply." Obviously, though, African Americans have had the worst of it by far.

Skin color and national background are completely irrelevant to job performance. They don't matter. What matters are traits like competence, character, and availability. So when we discriminate based on skin color we treat a difference that doesn't matter as if it does. That's wrong.

Just to make sure the point is clear, think about a case like this: Suppose you're the casting director for a movie—or no, let's make it two movies. One is about George Washington, the other about George Washington Carver. You have a line of actors waiting to try out for the two starring roles. Wouldn't you expect the lines to divide naturally, with African Americans heading toward one audition, whites toward the other, and no Asian Americans in sight? If a white man wanted to go up for the role of George Washington Carver, wouldn't you discriminate against him based on his skin color?

In that case the difference genuinely matters, so it's fine to treat it as if it does.

There are very few situations where sexual orientation matters for employment. Where it doesn't matter, it ought not come up. Where it does matter, it should. (One place it often does matter is in religious employment.) To my knowledge there is no valid research supporting the common misconception that gay men are more likely than straight men to be sexual predators in child care or classroom settings. For persons who do have an identifiable history of sexual offense, however, employment (and housing) discrimination can make good sense—whether they are straight or gay. That would be relevant, just discrimination.

What about marriage, though? Christians get accused of discrimination because we stand against gay marriage. Do we deserve that bad reputation? That depends on whether we've practiced just or unjust discrimination.

When it comes to marriage, the charge is that we've discriminated against gays, but that's not the case. Rather, we've discriminated between man–woman marriage and same-sex marriage. We've said that one of these is a time-tested, vitally important institution, and the other (as I've explained in chapters 3 and 4) is something else entirely.

Gays and lesbians have always been free to marry—there's never been any discrimination against them there. They just haven't been able to marry persons of the same sex. There really has been discrimination there, but it hasn't been against the *people*; it's been against the *institution* called same-sex marriage.

I know that answer might sound like trickery with words, since straight people have always been able to marry whomever they want, and gays and lesbians couldn't until recently. But is that seeing things accurately? I was talking with my daughter about this a while ago. She has a former boyfriend (I'll call him Jason) who isn't quite over her yet. I asked her, "Could Jason marry you?" She gave me a really sour look. I don't blame her. I deserved it! She got my point: straight men and women can't marry just anyone they want, either. Where would all the sad love songs and movies and TV shows be, if everyone married the person they wanted to marry and lived happily ever after?

Still, this probably sounds like a trick of logic. Straight people have at least been able to hope there was someone out there they would want to marry. For a long, long time, this was denied to gays and lesbians. For many of them it's been enormously painful. It has seemed unjust, and it has felt like discrimination. Straight people could marry, and they couldn't. Were they that much worse than straights that they should be locked out of being able to marry? Straight people never had to pass a moral test to get married, and surely many gays and lesbians are better citizens than many straights! Yet the system has always made them feel like lesser people. For many gays, it felt like unjust discrimination—but that was never the reality.

Let me say that again: It might have felt that way, but it never was true.

I felt the need to repeat that because it will probably come as a surprise to you, your teen, and anyone your teen would talk to. If it seemed like I was using trickery before, I'm definitely not using it now. The reality was never that gays and lesbians were denied marriage because anyone was discriminating against them as persons. No one denied them marriage because they were considered lesser human beings. They were denied same-sex marriage because everyone had always agreed that same-sex marriage wasn't really marriage.

There is discrimination there, no doubt, but it's been discrimination against the establishment of an institution called same-sex marriage, not discrimination against gays or lesbians as persons. In chapters 3 and 4, I wrote a host of reasons to consider it just, proper, and right for us to have discriminated that way.

Tips for Talking with Your Teen

You might say something like this to your teen, always bearing in mind that this isn't a script; it's a guide for discussion:

If someone says it's discrimination to deny gays the right to marry, your first crucial step is to listen actively, empathetically, and genuinely. There are real feelings involved.

Once you've genuinely connected with the person as a person, then you can go on to the next step. Try to make it clear that what we've been saying hasn't been, "You can't marry because you're not as good." We haven't been discriminating that way. What we've been trying to say is, "You can't marry someone of the same sex because that isn't marriage." Of course we've been overruled on that by the Supreme Court, and legally, same-sex couples can be married now. The court changed the meaning of marriage to make that possible.

Maybe now, though, you can at least see that we weren't discriminating against gays or lesbians as persons. We were discriminating against the formation of an institution—same-sex marriage—that has never made sense to us.

There are many reasons we say that. We know that the other side has reasons to disagree on it. For this, you're going to have to buckle down and do some actual study, I'm afraid. See chapters 3 and 4 for one place to start on that.

"We didn't choose to be gay."

The Challenge

"It's unjust for you to hold something against us that we didn't choose. It's a part of who we are, it's not by choice, so how is it immoral to act according to who we are?"

Truths Your Teen Needs to Know

Most LGBT individuals report discovering their sexual preference at an early age. Very few of them welcomed the discovery when they made it, so it would be wrong to say they chose it for themselves. If they want to convince us that "not choosing it" makes their desires right, it won't do the job for them. Inborn/unchosen desires can be wrong, too.

Digging Deeper

There's a false assumption underlying this challenge: if we're born with a fault or picked it up through no intention of our own, it can't be sinful to act it out. If that were true, people with a genetic tendency toward alcoholism couldn't be blamed for repeatedly getting drunk. We can empathize with their plight, but we wouldn't tell them their drunkenness is just fine, would we? Being born a certain way doesn't automatically make it okay to act that way.

We all have inborn personality leanings. Some of us, for example, are naturally more aggressive than others. That doesn't make it okay to act out all our impulses. Every parent knows that their children's moments of anger and selfishness aren't okay just because they were born with those tendencies.

Therefore, while it's important for us to listen and empathize when someone says, "I didn't choose to be LGBT," that fact alone doesn't have anything to do with whether acting it out is right or wrong.

Christians believe we're all born with a sin problem. Each of us expresses it in different ways. It's in all of us. That certainly doesn't change sin into non-sin.

Tips for Talking with Your Teen

You might say something like this to your teen, always bearing in mind that this isn't a script; it's a guide for discussion:

If there was ever a time to listen to what an LGBT person says, this would be it. They're opening up their heart to you. Treat it well. Don't rush to answer, but look to God for your timing.

When it's time to answer, use the alcohol connection [explained in "Digging Deeper"] to show there's a weakness in this objection. Take it slowly and sensitively, though. They've probably heard it before, and chances are they don't like it. That's not because the point it makes is false, but because it's really uncomfortable for them to face. It wouldn't be unusual for them to miss your point, as in, "What? Are you saying that what we're doing is like being an alcoholic?" Your answer to that would be, "No, that's not what I meant by it. I only wanted to show you that 'I was born this way' doesn't make it right."

That still gets you into emotionally sensitive areas, and it's likely to put them on the defensive. You might find it's more helpful to speak first about the biblical view that all sin is inborn for all of us.

Either way, this whole topic opens up layers upon layers of feelings and reasons. Don't rush into trying to settle it, and don't feel like you need to win an argument here. Listen well and be a friend. You can stick with your principles in the process if you're sensitive in the way you do it.

"We can't help who we love, so why not let us love them?"

The Challenge

"We can't help who we love, so why not let us be free to love them?"

Truths Your Teen Needs to Know

Love isn't exclusive to marriage or to sexual relationships.

Digging Deeper

There are many ways to love, not all of them sexual. Sometimes the possibility of a sexual relationship actually hinders love.

For many people that statement will come as quite a surprise. That's because more and more, over the past fifty years or so, our culture has made it seem like there's no such thing as love without sex. In a brilliant 2010 *Touchstone* article titled "Sanity and Matrimony," Anthony Esolen showed how false that really is. His view was that same-sex marriage would

> curtail opportunities for deep and emotionally fulfilling friendships between members of the same sex, opportunities that are already few and strained. . . .
>
> Boys in particular now suffer a pincers attack. The sexual revolution rouses them to interest, or to the pretense of interest, in girls long before they or the girls are emotionally or intellectually ready for it; and now the condoning of homosexuality prevents them from publicly preferring the company of their own sex. This is simply inarguable. If a George Gershwin nowadays shows up at Maxie Rosenzweig's house all the time, while his pals are outside on the streets playing stickball, then there must be something up with George and Maxie.
>
> If you do not think that this is the way teens and even children now talk, then you are not paying attention. What was once innocent, or what both Maxie and George need never have worried about, now means something. Unless they are

comfortable with the meaning, they will shy away from one another; the friendship will not deepen. Confess, reader: if you come upon two teenage boys in a pond skinny-dipping, it is the first thing you will think, and you will think it despite the fact that before bathing suits were invented, it was the only way two boys could ever be found swimming.[9]

Thus some gay-rights advocates have concluded, based on absolutely no evidence, that the biblical David and Jonathan's deep covenant love for each other was probably sexual. Our culture's obsession with sex has made it hard to think of love in any other way. "Love" has been restricted, its meaning sharply limited to include romance and familial love and almost nothing else. The LGBT revolution has supposedly advanced "love," permitting gay men and lesbians to love one another sexually, but at the same time it's put up a new barrier in front of anyone loving same-sex friends nonsexually.

Here's a better way to view it. To stand against homosexuality is not to oppose same-sex friendship or love, but rather to say that *sexual expressions* of same-sex love violate God's best plan for men and women. So if the question is, "Why not let us love?" the answer is, we're not standing in the way of love. We believe in love. We believe it can exist apart from sex. There's one relationship where sex is appropriate—between a married man and woman—but there are many relationships, including ordinary friendship, in which love can flourish without sex.

We recognize that this leaves romantically attracted same-sex couples in a difficult place, and we want to be sensitive to the pain that entails. There is a group of writers who understand: the celibate Christian gays and lesbians writing at spiritualfriendship.org, who have acknowledged their sexual preferences and yet have determined to follow biblical principles, abstaining from sex apart from opposite-sex marriage.

---

9. Anthony Esolen, "Sanity and Matrimony: Ten Arguments in Defense of Marriage (Part 1 of 2)," *Touchstone*, July/August 2010, www.touchstonemag.com/archives /article.php?id=23-04-028-f.

Meanwhile some of us can also attest to years of living in chastity as single persons. We know it's a challenge. We also know that living God's way is best.

We in the church need to be believable on this, though. Decades of heterosexual running around, even in the church, have hurt our credibility. You and I can't solve the promiscuity problem ourselves, but we can resolve to live with integrity, including being willing to sacrifice and deny ourselves for Christ's sake.

Tips for Talking with Your Teen

You might say something like this to your teen, always bearing in mind that this isn't a script; it's a guide for discussion:

This question is drenched with feelings, including pain and anger. Be sure to listen well. The great writer and thinker Francis Schaeffer used to speak of weeping with those who are coming face-to-face with the often disturbing truths of God. This might be one of those times.

I can't imagine wanting another man in a physical relationship, but I can imagine that if two men wanted one another that way and if they were starting to face the fact that it could be wrong to fulfill their desires, they would really be torn between what they wanted and what they thought to be right. We're asking men and women to face that kind of pain head-on. It isn't something to treat lightly.

What if the people you're talking with aren't dealing with it that way, though? What if they think you're the one who's wrong? They might be angry at you. At that point, what they would need to hear from you most would be that you care, even if they're angry; but that you're also bound by your convictions and God's Word. It wasn't your idea to set the limits God set.

When the right time comes, share how you know that God is good in spite of what seem to be limits he's set on us. You can find relevant information on that in chapters 3 and 4 of this book. His goodness is most obviously demonstrated through Jesus Christ, who endured intense pain and grief himself in his trial and crucifixion and did it for all of us.

The way of the cross is a way of self-denial and at the same time a way of entering into the eternal joy of Jesus Christ. It's worth it!

"Same-sex marriage takes nothing away from traditional marriage."

The Challenge

"Same-sex marriage doesn't take anything away from anyone's traditional marriage. Why worry about what other people are doing when they're not hurting you with it?"

Truths Your Teen Needs to Know

A couple's marriage is a private matter, but only to an extent. The overall institution of marriage is a matter of public concern. Strong families thrive best in a culture that supports and encourages them. Support of that sort has been waning over the past several decades. As I argue below (and also in chapter 2, in the section titled "Setting the Stage"), same-sex marriage wasn't originally the cause of that decline. It's becoming a major contributor to it, though.

Digging Deeper

"No man is an island," wrote John Donne. No couple is an island, either. While it's true that each marriage stands or falls on its own strength, marriages also tend to gain or lose strength, on the whole, based on how well the surrounding culture supports them.

Marriage culture in the Western world has been eroding since at least the 1960s. Same-sex marriage is both a symptom of and a contributor to that decline. It's a *symptom* in that no one would have even thought of it, had marriage not been as severely undermined as it has been over the past several decades (see chapter 2). Because marriage lost its unique meaning for so many, it reached the point that it could mean anything at all. In this sense, same-sex marriage is just one symptom of a much larger problem. But it's also become a *contributor* to the problem by enshrining in law and custom the latest watered-down version of marriage-that-can-mean-anything.

I'm convinced that this has been largely fueled by the idea that marriage exists for the couple's personal satisfaction. It's the "just you and me, babe" view of marriage I wrote about earlier. As this view has crept across our culture, it has directly damaged the real institution of marriage built upon "you and me and the kids we expect, and the community we'll be building together."

Thus on one view, marriage is a lifelong project of rich, enduring relationships, deeply rewarding yet often requiring significant sacrifice. The message of "just you and me, babe" marriage, in contrast—including many straight relationships and the majority of LGBT relationships—is that it need not involve the same sacrifice. Some sacrifice, yes, but nothing like the sacrifice of raising children. People want marriage to be easy and comfortable; and if it ceases being that, then it's disposable.

Thus while married men and women work through the trying turbulence of raising kids and loving one another, they're hammered with the message that it could be so much easier: all they have to do is let loose of all the trouble and focus instead on what satisfies themselves. Lacking social support to stick with marriage through a challenging season, too often they back out. They separate. They divorce.

Gay marriage isn't the cause of all this, but it's a huge stamp of approval on the unhealthy principle behind it. Therefore our stand against it has been just one front in the fight for a return to a healthy marriage culture, along with massive (though less visible) church-based efforts to strengthen existing marriages, prevent divorce, and support healthy parenting.

So this question has both a quick answer and a much longer one. The quick answer goes like this: Does same-sex marriage take anything away from natural marriage? Yes. It undermines the culture that motivates marriages to stay together, that helps keep men with women and women with men for the benefit of their children and their communities. The longer answer includes a full explanation of why that's so, and why it matters.

Unlike some of the other topics in this part of the book, I can't think of an easy way to boil that down to a few pithy conversational points. It's deeply wrapped up in the most important question of the day: What is marriage? I don't mean, what is marriage according to the court, but, what is marriage, rightly understood? (For we still think there's a difference.) There's only one way you or your teen will be able to answer that question well: by developing a solid grasp on what marriage is meant to be—*and why.* That was the point of chapters 2 through 4 of this book, which you might want to reread. Have your teen read them, too. Even that information just scratches the surface. For further study, I suggest you go to the resource guide in the back of this book and look up the writings by Sean McDowell and John Stonestreet, Michael Brown, or the team of writers including Sherif Girgis, Ryan Anderson, and Robert George.

Tips for Talking with Your Teen

You might say something like this to your teen, always bearing in mind that this isn't a script; it's a guide for discussion:

There's an easy answer to this question and a harder one. The easy one is that same-sex marriage is more of the same kind of thing that's been happening for decades, and that has been hurting children badly, including a lot of your friends. I'm talking about everything that makes it less likely for moms and dads to see how important their marriage is to their kids, so that they'll work hard to keep their marriage strong. When marriage is mostly about the couple, and the couple decides they don't like being together any longer, what do they do? Too often they give it up. That's the problem with a lot of marriages today. It's a result of marriages being for "just you and me, babe," which is generally what same-sex marriage is all about.

So depending on what your friend's family situation is like, you can share those thoughts and then ask them whether they'd like it if their parents looked at their marriage that way. Or, depending on their family again, consider asking, "Don't you wish your parents had seen their marriage as being about more than just each other?"

That's the short answer. The rest of it is harder. It's the whole marriage issue wrapped up in one question. To answer it really well, you need to have at least some grasp on the whole answer.

I'd like you to study and learn that answer. Reading the first part of this book will get you started. In the meantime, if someone asks you to say more about this, there may be nothing better for you to say than, "Look, I've done some work on this, and honestly it's a tough issue. I have to admit I don't have the answers clear enough in my head to explain them to you right now. It's like the difference between knowing something, and knowing it well enough to teach it. I know it, but not well enough to explain it."

Then come back and read the first part of Critical Conversations.

Or, if you think this is more personally honest, consider saying, "I've got a lot to learn about this, honestly, but I'm getting good information from people—my parents and my church—who have been trustworthy on a lot of things, and I'm willing to trust them for now on this, too. I'm going to do my own study on this, and I'm going to make my own decisions. Until then, I'm sticking with the people I know I can trust." That's riskier than the first answer, since your friends aren't always going to understand why you trust the people you do, and they might even laugh at you for it. I want you to be honest, though, so answer whichever way fits you best.

"Gay and lesbian couples can be just as good parents as straight couples."

The Challenge

"You talk about marriage being important for building the next generation. Why won't you let gay and lesbian couples take part in it? Gay and lesbian couples can be just as good parents as straight couples."

Truths Your Teen Needs to Know

We know that children raised by their own mom and dad in a loving relationship do very well, on the whole. We also know that same-sex couples can adopt children, and we know they can be loving and nurturing parents. We do not know, however, in spite of loud claims that research has proven it, that children do as well being raised by same-sex parents as they do with opposite-sex parents.

Digging Deeper

Can gay and lesbian couples raise children to the same level of emotional, physical, relational, and spiritual maturity as straight couples? That's a matter of intense controversy. Both sides of the debate can quote research studies in their favor. Both sides can explain how the other side's studies are flawed.

For most of us it looks like a standoff. How are we supposed to know who's right and who's wrong? That's a technical question, unfortunately, and most of the people staking out positions on it are unequipped to draw the conclusions they've drawn. I hold an MS degree in psychology (Industrial and Organizational) with a strong research emphasis included. I know how to read the research. I find the data less than overwhelmingly clear on either side. The best (though still not definitive) research suggests that LGBT homes have not proven to be great environments for children. These studies unfortunately lack the statistical power to show exactly which factors, among many possible ones, are most to blame for those outcomes.[10]

---

10. The best research study so far, in my opinion, is a multi-dataset analysis by Donald Paul Sullins. Released early in 2015, his study indicates that emotional

So some of the science on this is not terribly clear. This much is clear, though: there's a *lot* of research supporting the positive results of growing up in a family led by one's own mom and dad in a loving relationship. We know that that kind of relationship works well for children, generally speaking. We do *not* know that raising children under a same-sex couple's parentage works as well. Anyone who claims they do know is guilty of an ideologically driven rush to judgment.

That's a strong statement, but I stand by it. As I wrote in chapter 2, *all* of the research on this is still preliminary, and it will remain that way for at least the next twenty to forty years—because this huge social experiment's results won't be known until we see how it all comes out in the children of the children now being raised in same-sex households.

There's a further, broader issue that enters into this at the same time. The rise of gay marriage is bound to undermine the one form of parenting that's definitely known to be good for children. (I cover that effect in chapter 2 and also in the topic, "Same-sex marriage takes nothing away from traditional marriage.")

So the claim that gay and lesbian couples can be just as good parents is doubtful at best. Meanwhile, there is good reason to believe that gay-rights activism is undermining what's good for children across our entire society.

Tips for Talking with Your Teen

What follows here might or might not be enough to help your teen catch the point well enough that they could explain it. If it is, great; if

---

problems are twice as frequent among children raised by same-sex couples. Like other research of its type, his work has been heavily criticized, essentially for comparing apples and oranges (different relationship situations between same-sex and opposite-sex couples). My view on it is that it's more like comparing tangerines and oranges: not a perfect one-to-one comparison, but close enough that we can safely begin to say that research seems to indicate that same-sex couples' children do less well than children of opposite-sex couples. D. Paul Sullins, "Emotional Problems Among Children with Same-Sex Parents: Difference by Definition," *British Journal of Education, Society & Behavioural Science* 7, no. 2 (2015).

not, I suggest you spend some time with your teen talking about what I've written here under "Digging Deeper." Either way you might say something like this to your teen, always bearing in mind that this isn't a script; it's a guide for discussion:

It's too early: no one could possibly know whether gay and lesbian couples will prove in general to be as good parents for their children as straight couples generally are. When someone says they are, just ask them, "What about their children? How will they do as parents? How will their children turn out?" There's no answer because nobody knows yet.

That leads to the obvious follow-up question: "How can we be so sure that children do as well in same-sex households when we don't have a clue how they're going to do as parents themselves? Don't you think that's an important part of the question?"

If that's not enough to help them understand what the problems are with what they're saying, I suggest you let them know that the scientists who study these things haven't really come to agreement on it. Then ask, "What are your qualifications for deciding whose research is right and whose is wrong?"

"What's done in the privacy of someone else's bedroom is none of your business."

The Challenge

"Why are you so concerned over this issue, anyway? What people do in the privacy of their bedrooms is none of your business."

Truths Your Teen Needs to Know

It was gay-rights activists who brought this controversy into the public sphere. When they made it a public concern, that's exactly what it became: a public concern.

Digging Deeper

LGBT culture was never just a matter of bedroom privacy. Ever since the famous 1969 Stonewall Riots in New York City, which is commonly considered to be the founding moment in the gay-rights movement, this has been a public concern. Since then, as we saw in chapter 2, activists have attempted unrelentingly to keep it in the public eye. So this slogan is really quite disingenuous. It's not the private activities in people's bedrooms we're concerned about. It's all the public campaigns, ranging from local gay pride parades to major legislative battles.

Tips for Talking with Your Teen

There's a very quick, easy answer for this challenge. "Fine. Now, can we get back on topic, please? Because we're really not all that concerned with what happens in people's bedrooms. We have other matters to attend to."

"Stop imposing your religious beliefs on us!"

The Challenge
"Don't impose your religious beliefs on us."

Truths Your Teen Needs to Know
Imposing is a loaded term that doesn't describe very well what we've been trying to do. Before the Supreme Court legalized gay marriage, we were participating in the same democratic process as everyone else. Since then we've continued to stand for our beliefs within that same democratic process.

Digging Deeper
No Christian has ever imposed religious beliefs about gay marriage on anyone through any political process. Sure, we've brought our beliefs to the table for discussion. We've campaigned according to our beliefs and values. *That's what everyone does.* No law or moral principle has ever said we couldn't vote according to our beliefs. We've won some and we've lost some. That's how democracies work. In the end, the Supreme Court told us no. That's how our government works sometimes, too.

We aren't demanding anyone obey the Bible who doesn't believe in it. God will hold them accountable for that, not us. Besides, we can make our case for marriage without even appealing to God, the Bible, or religion. That's what most of chapter 3 in this book was about.[11]

But I wouldn't want to communicate the wrong thing here. Suppose the only reasons I had for my position were religious ones. Would I still feel the freedom to stand for my beliefs? Of course I would! In fact, I'd feel a strong *obligation* to stand for them. But our reasons aren't only religious. God's moral commands are for our relational,

11. See also Sherif Girgis, Robert George, and Ryan T. Anderson, "What Is Marriage?" *Harvard Journal of Law and Public Policy* 34, no. 1 (2010); Sherif Girgis, Ryan T. Anderson, and Robert George, *What Is Marriage? Man and Woman: A Defense* (New York: Encounter Books, 2012).

moral, spiritual, and emotional good. We can speak of their goodness, and, where appropriate, we can do so without even mentioning
God or the Bible. We can make our case on secular grounds or religious grounds. Either way, American democracy gives us every right
to make our case, and we can still make it today.

Finally, there's something fundamentally wrong with this slogan.
It comes across as telling religious people to keep out of the marriage
debate, or at least to keep our beliefs out. My response to that is simply, "No, thank you, I think we all have the right to be involved."

Tips for Talking with Your Teen

You might say something like this to your teen, always bearing in
mind that this isn't a script; it's a guide for discussion:

*When someone challenges you over this, respond by reminding them,
"This is a democracy. Sure, Christians tried to get our views put into law,
but how is that different from what everyone else does in a democracy?"*

*That ought to settle it. Sometimes, though, people will say there's
something wrong with it just because your views are religious. They've
gotten this idea from what they've heard about the separation of church
and state. You don't need to worry about whether that's getting the First
Amendment right or wrong. Just ask, "Suppose we came to the table with
nonreligious reasons for our position. We can do that, you know. Would
you still say we were imposing our religion on you?"*

*They might answer yes. If so, what they're saying is that if you have a
religious side to you, you can't take part in politics, even if you keep quiet
about your religion. Now, let's look at the First Amendment again. Does
it tell religious people we have to keep quiet in politics?*

*Be patient in conversations like this. Sometimes when people think
we're pushing our beliefs on them, they get annoyed, upset, or even angry
about it. I encourage you to take time to listen and understand in the
course of your conversations. Pray while you talk. If they get upset, stay
strong in the calm confidence of your position, and if they move in the
direction of anger, don't follow them there.*

GROUP C: REGARDING GOD AND THE BIBLE

The rest of the challenges in this book deal with Christians' belief in God and the Bible. As we enter this section, I'd like to give you some general coaching you can pass along to your teen.

First, frequently I find that although these challenges may seem to come out of the Bible, their real source is usually the atheist Internet where there's not much Bible knowledge at all. Someone may write a blog post, for example, saying that the Bible teaches all different kinds of marriage (one of our topics below). That distorted information gets circulated and repeated. A challenger hears about it and raises the question, thinking it's a genuine, Bible-based problem, when in fact it's the product of ignorance.

I've often been tempted to be blunt: "You know, that's just totally ignorant. You don't have the slightest idea what you're talking about"— because honestly, they *don't* have a clue. If I said that I wouldn't be wrong, and yet I would be. It wouldn't get me any closer to my goal, which isn't to prove I'm right but to help the person appreciate and accept the truth in Christ. We can't afford to forget what we're really trying to accomplish. A patient, winsomely presented answer is usually better than a quick contradiction. (Sadly, I sometimes forget that.)

Second, all these questions are on biblical turf, so in every case, a biblical answer is appropriate. The people who raise these challenges don't always get that. Here's how the discussion often goes instead. The questioner starts out with something like, "You say you believe the Bible, but what about this strange thing I think the Bible teaches here?"

We begin to answer, explaining what the Bible is really teaching there. Then our challenger shifts the question on us, saying something like, "The Bible is an outmoded book of fairy tales," or even, "The Bible is homophobic."

That's called changing the subject. At that point I'd ask if they want to hear my answer to their question about what the Bible teaches or not.

Third, I've had people tell me I couldn't use the Bible as my information source since they don't believe in it. I once had a long debate with someone about the meaning of the word *faith*. I pointed out that for two thousand years, the meaning of *faith* has been overwhelmingly influenced by the way the Bible uses the word. Since obviously the Bible is relevant to how our culture has understood faith, I began to explain to him just how the authors of the Bible used the term, at which point he answered, "I don't believe in the Bible, so you can't use it here." I wondered, *What? The Bible is the main source of information on how Western culture uses the word* faith. *Am I not allowed to look in the Bible to find out what the Bible says?* Don't be fooled by tactics like that.

This means, by the way, that for some of these questions you and your teen will need to have your Bible open in front of you, exploring specific passages together. Your teen will need to use the Bible with his or her friends in the same way. It's a great Scripture learning opportunity.

Those are three general tips for dealing with biblically based objections to Christian morality. Now for specifics.

"Jesus never spoke out against homosexuality."

The Challenge
"If homosexuality is wrong, why didn't Jesus speak out against it?"

Truths Your Teen Needs to Know
Jesus didn't speak out against rape, bestiality, incest, stalking, or a lot of things we know are wrong, yet he did strongly affirm marriage between a man and a woman.

Digging Deeper
It's wrong to conclude that some moral law is unimportant just because we don't have any record of Jesus talking about it. He didn't

mention rape, incest, or bestiality, either. Why didn't he? My guess is, he didn't need to: it was already clear enough!

Not only that, but Christians don't believe Jesus's "red-letter" words are more inspired than the rest of Scripture. Properly understood and interpreted, it's *all* true, and it's all equally the Word of God.

Jesus did speak clearly about marriage, though. He was actually very specific about it:

> And Pharisees came up to him and tested him by asking, "Is it lawful to divorce one's wife for any cause?" He answered, "Have you not read that he who created them from the beginning made them male and female, and said, 'Therefore a man shall leave his father and his mother and hold fast to his wife, and the two shall become one flesh'? So they are no longer two but one flesh. What therefore God has joined together, let not man separate." (Matt. 19:3–6)

There's no hint that Jesus thought of marriage being anything but what it had always been: a man leaving his parents and joining his wife, and the two becoming one flesh.

Some pro-LGBT people take Jesus's silence on homosexuality to extremes that are both obviously wrong and also quite disturbing. They say, for example, that Jesus supported homosexuality by healing the centurion's servant in Matthew 8:5–13. This servant was really the Roman official's boy-lover, they say, and Jesus healed him in support of that relationship.[1] This is demonstrably false.[2] It's also considerably milder than some other, really disturbing examples I could tell about. It just goes to show how far some people will stretch facts to suit their preferences.

---

1. "Jesus Affirmed a Gay Couple," Would Jesus Discriminate? website, accessed July 19, 2014, www.wouldjesusdiscriminate.org/biblical_evidence/gay_couple.html.
2. Denny Burk, "Did Jesus Affirm a Gay Couple?" blog, September 10, 2010, www .dennyburk.com/did-jesus-affirm-a-gay-couple/.

Tips for Talking with Your Teen

You might say something like this to your teen, always bearing in mind that this isn't a script; it's a guide for discussion:

When a friend asks you about this, a good place to begin is by asking, "Did Jesus speak out against rape?" They might not know the answer, so feel free to help them along. When your friend realizes the answer is no, go ahead and ask, "Does that mean Jesus thought rape was no big deal?"

Then point out how Jesus did think marriage was a big deal. If you have a Bible app on your phone—or a printed Bible nearby—go ahead and look up Matthew 19:3–6. If not, just paraphrase it, and tell them Jesus said that marriage was important from the beginning, it was for a man and a woman from the beginning, and it was always meant to last.

"If God is love, why would he be opposed to committed, loving relationships?"

The Challenge
"Christians believe God is love. Why would he stand in the way of two people's love, just because they're the same sex?"

Truths Your Teen Needs to Know
Love isn't all that's true of God, and not everything that goes by the name of love is a true expression of God's love.

Digging Deeper
This challenge invokes a supposed contradiction: God is supposedly loving, but you're telling LGBT people, "Don't love."

No, in fact, that's not what we're telling them at all. We're trying to be clear on what God's love really is.

Not everything that goes by the name *love* deserves to be called that. Some of us are old enough to remember San Francisco's "Summer of Love" in the 1960s. It was misnamed; more accurately, it was a summer of sex. There's a "Man–Boy Love Association" for men who have a certain perverted preference. They call it "love," but it's far from the real thing. Love is an easy word to misuse.

And this question is about God's love in particular. Yes, God is a God of love. He's also a God of holiness, justice, mercy, wisdom, truth, and much more—all of which are true of God in full measure, without contradiction. They aren't balanced against each other, as if more holiness meant less love or more justice meant less grace. All these facets of God's character come together in fullness and in unity. God's love is completely just, merciful, wise, true, holy, and so on. Therefore any love that fails to fulfill any of his other attributes isn't God's love. If there is some so-called love that's unwise, it's not God's love. If there is love that's not holy, it's not God's love. God is in no way bound to approve everything with the name *love* on it, but only love that expresses his complete character and lines up with his entire loving will.

We're not standing in the way of same-sex love, at any rate. Two people of the same sex can love one another with a godly love. The Bible tells us of David and Jonathan's deep covenant love for each other. Truly loving same-sex friendship is (generally speaking) truly good—provided that it does not include the unholiness of a physical, sexual relationship. (You can read more about same-sex love under the topic, "We can't help who we love, so why not let us love them?")

We affirm God's love. We affirm friendship and same-sex love, as long at it's a true expression of God's holy character.

Tips for Talking with Your Teen

You might say something like this to your teen, always bearing in mind that this is a guide for discussion, not a script:

If a friend brings up this challenge with you, the core of your response should be, "Not everything that goes by the name of love really is love." Everybody knows that's true. All you need to do is help the other person realize they believe it.

To make that point clear, ask, "Do you believe that everything that goes by the name of 'love' really is love?" If they can't think of an example, offer them this one: "What about a stalker's so-called love?"

That ought to help them understand that "love" isn't always really love.

Count on it, though: your friend is very likely to say that a man's love for a man is different, and so is a woman's love for a woman.

But remember where this particular question comes from. It's about God. They're saying that God ought to consider same-sex physical desire to be love. That raises the question, how would they know that about God? Everyone has an opinion, but do they really know what God's own view is on this? More often than not, their view of God comes from their own private interpretations of whatever religious opinions they've run across. It's their own beliefs about God. You could explore that by asking, "You say that if we deny homosexuality we're denying God's love. Tell me: how would we know whether it was God's love or not?"

If they're ready to answer, then you've just gotten started on a conversation about how people know the truth about God. Stick with that conversation. Take it slow, be patient, listen well, and stick with it as long as they're willing to stay in it with you. Offer to bring them to Bible study with you. It doesn't have to be about LGBT issues; in fact, it's much better if it isn't. After all, the idea is to think about how we know what's true of God.

Meanwhile, remind them it's too early for them to say Christianity contradicts God's love. They're in the process of finding out what God is really like, and they don't know enough about him to make that judgment. Either that, or they've refused to get involved in finding out what God is really like. In that case, they really have no business judging him!

"God made me this way, so how could it be wrong?"

The Challenge

"God made me gay [or lesbian, bi, or trans]. How could it be wrong to live the way he made me?"

Truths Your Teen Needs to Know

God made humans in his image, but because of sin, we're no longer what God intended us to be. We can't use what we *feel we are* as a signpost toward what we *ought to do*.

Digging Deeper

When Adam and Eve sinned, they fell from perfect fellowship with God. Ever since then, we humans haven't been what we were meant to be. We've lost our innocence, we've lost our close connection with God, and we've been stained with evil. Just look around you; it's easy to see that no one is totally on track in life.

People are born with different problems. We pick up different challenges as we go through our lives. Some of these problems are physical, some are in our personalities and character. No sensible person says his character flaws are good just because "God made me this way." If that were true, then anything could be right, including any strong, seemingly irresistible preference for anything at all, just because "that's the way God made me." Alcoholism would be right because "that's the way God made me." An out-of-control anger issue would be right because "that's the way God made me."

The difference between good and bad isn't based on where our preferences came from or how strong they are. After all, the Bible has a word for many of our strongest, most seemingly irresistible preferences. That word is *temptation*.

Tips for Talking with Your Teen

You might say something like this to your teen, always bearing in mind that this isn't a script; it's a guide for discussion:

As you answer this, remember some people honestly don't understand God or the Bible, and you want to draw them toward God, not away from him, while also answering the challenge. Questions are a powerful yet gentle way to show them they must be wrong. You can open with something like, "Tell me about the God you think made you this way." Then follow up with questions:

> *How do you know that's what that God intended? Where did you find that out about God?*

> *Do you think it's generally true that, "I was made this way," means, "It must be right"? Can you think of anyone who could say, "I was made this way," and yet have something be wrong about the way they are?"*

Your friend shouldn't have any trouble thinking of examples, but if they do, remind them of inborn traits some people suffer from. Some mental illnesses are connected to genetics—does that make acting out on one's impulses right and good?

That ought to settle this challenge.

"Marriage in the Bible wasn't always one man with one woman."

The Challenge
"You say marriage is supposed to be for a man and a woman, but your Bible has all kinds of different marriages than that."

Truths Your Teen Needs to Know
The Bible strongly affirms monogamy. Other forms of marriage consistently end up being bad examples. And all of the marriages in the Bible (yes, even the polygamous ones) were between men and women.

Digging Deeper
The Bible tells stories of polygamy, incestuous marriages, men keeping concubines, and even worse relationships. It tells the stories honestly enough—and virtually all of them turn out to be bad examples. Scripture says these kinds of marriage happened; it doesn't say they were good.

Abraham's polygamous relationship with Hagar produced Ishmael, whose descendants have been Israel's enemies for untold generations (see Gen. 16). Jacob had multiple wives, resulting in a jealous band of half-brothers whose infighting led them to sell one of their own into slavery (Gen. 37:18–36). David's dalliance with Bathsheba was a sinful abuse of power; their first son was taken from them in death (2 Sam. 12). Solomon had hundreds of wives and concubines in blatant disobedience to God's command (Deut. 17:14–17; 1 Kings 11:1–13). His sons fought among themselves, with the result that the kingdom was divided (1 Kings 12).

I could go on. The record is consistent: nonmonogamous marriages turned out poorly.

Not only that, but marriage in the Bible was always man-and-woman. Where there was polygamy, each marriage was between male and female. The women weren't married to each other. Men were never married to men.

So while the Old Testament *reports* multiple forms of marriage, what it *affirms*—what it really teaches—is to "rejoice in the wife of your youth" (Prov. 5:18; Eccl. 9:9; and no, it wasn't advising women to do that).

There are no multiple marriages in the New Testament. It's always singular, never plural: "the husband" and "the wife" (e.g., Eph. 5:22–23). A church leader—as pacesetter and example for the rest of the church—is to be a "one-woman man," as some have paraphrased the "husband of one wife" instruction in Titus 1:6 and 1 Timothy 3:2.

This wasn't a new discovery in New Testament days. It was that way from the beginning: "A man shall leave his father and his mother and hold fast to his wife, and they shall become one flesh" (Gen. 2:24). This is what the Bible teaches.

Tips for Talking with Your Teen

You might say something like this to your teen, always bearing in mind that this isn't a script; it's a guide for discussion:

Keep in mind that the person who raises this challenge probably doesn't know much about what's in the Bible. A good place to start, then, might be, "Would you like to know what the Bible actually says about that?"

If your friend answers yes, then take the time to go through some of the passages provided here. If time is short, summarize what the passages say. (Treat the person's interest with care as you do so. Don't smother them with more than they're ready for. As they say in show business, "Always leave them wanting more.")

Of course they might tell you they don't really want to hear what's in the Bible. Then you might as well call it like it is: they've jumped to a conclusion, without caring to find out whether they have their facts straight. Ask them whether they think that's a good way to look at things. Maybe they'll come around. If not, there's not much you can do but pray and try to stay friends with them anyway.

"Why do you say no to homosexuality, and yet eat shellfish and wear mixed fabrics?"

The Challenge

"The same Bible book that prohibits homosexuality—Leviticus— also forbids eating shellfish and wearing clothes of mixed fabric. Why do you insist on obeying one command while ignoring the others?"

Truths Your Teen Needs to Know

Some Old Testament commands were intended to be permanent, some were meant for only a season, and it's not hard to tell the difference.

Digging Deeper

This is one of the most common challenges out there. It's circulating widely on the Internet and in the media. I'm convinced it doesn't come from people who know the Bible, but from people who have heard it from someone who heard it from someone who heard it from someone, etc.

So how do we answer all these "someones"? To start with, this challenge could be stated in even harsher terms (and frequently it is). *Why don't we stone children for dishonoring their parents? Why don't we kill daughters who aren't virgins on their wedding night?* These commands are in the Old Testament, too. The same answers apply to all these challenges, so I'll focus on just a couple of them.

Leviticus 18:22 says, "You shall not lie with a male as with a woman; it is an abomination." Leviticus also says (19:19), "You shall not sow your field with two kinds of seed, nor shall you wear a garment of cloth made of two kinds of material." Leviticus 11:9–12 prohibits eating lobster and shrimp. Why then do we say everyone has to obey one of those commandments, but not the others?

Here's why. There are basically three kinds of law in the Old Testament: *moral, ceremonial,* and *civil.* The *moral law* is expressed most famously in the Ten Commandments, although it extends well beyond those ten crucial laws. It includes positive, enduring principles like the importance of worshiping God, loving God and others, caring for neighbors and strangers, and so on. It also includes prohibitions against evils like theft, murder, sexual immorality, injustice, and greed. The *ceremonial law* had to do with religious practice: sacrifices, prayers, feasts, and the like. The New Testament book of Hebrews explains how Jesus fulfilled the ceremonial law, bringing it to its intended end, thus making its regulations obsolete. Food laws in particular were put to an end, as shown in Mark 7:19 and Acts 10.

The *civil law* was essentially the code by which these rules were to be handled by civil authorities. It provided specific legal definitions and specific punishments for infractions. It was intended specifically for the nation of Israel. Although the *basic principles* underlying Israel's civil law have been studied and followed (more or less) by other nations since then, the Bible never suggests that the specifics in it should be the rule for every nation throughout all time.

The fact is, of these three, only the moral code was intended to be permanent. Its enduring nature is shown in at least three ways.

First, it's based in what God made humans to be. Because we are in his image, murder is wrong (Gen. 9:6–7). Because he created marriage to be what it is, right from the start (Gen. 1:26–27; 2:18–25), sexual immorality is wrong.

Second, God never held other nations accountable to Israel's civil law, and though he invited other nations' individuals to take part in Israel's ceremonial law, he didn't require it. When it came to the moral law, however, he was absolutely definite about it: he expected all nations, not just Israel, to obey. God judged the Canaanites for their idol worship and their sexual immorality, so we know those categories of law weren't just for Israel.

Third, the commands in the moral law were reaffirmed in the New Testament but never the civil and ceremonial laws.

Which category did "mixed fabrics" fit in? Was it moral, ceremonial, or civil? We don't really know fully what it was about. My guess is it was ceremonial: that the mixing of fabrics may have been a symbol for the mixing of religious beliefs. I know this much for sure: there's no reason to think it was part of any enduring moral law.

Tips for Talking with Your Teen

You might say something like this to your teen, always bearing in mind that this isn't a script; it's a guide for discussion:

This challenge simply requires explanation: some laws were meant to be permanent, others weren't. There's nothing contradictory about following the permanent ones and setting aside the temporary ones.

That's one way to answer. There's another one called "returning the burden of proof." It may sound complicated but it isn't. All it means is that if someone says you're interpreting the Bible incorrectly, they're more or less claiming to understand how to interpret it correctly. If so, then they should be able to prove it!

Here's one way to return the burden of proof. First, ask, "Do you think the Bible is contradictory on this?" Then ask, "Why? What's wrong with some laws lasting longer than others?" Very few challengers will know how to answer that. After all, there is nothing wrong with it.

That does not mean, however, that we must think every law is temporary. The laws about sexual morality were given to all nations, not just Israel; they're based in what it means to be human; and they're repeated in the New Testament. It's clear they were meant to last.

"The New Testament isn't talking about committed, monogamous same-sex marriage."

The Challenge

The New Testament condemns the kind of same-sex relationships that were known at the time, but that didn't include committed, monogamous same-sex relationships, since they hadn't been heard of then. Therefore same-sex marriage wasn't prohibited in the Bible.

Truths Your Teen Needs to Know

This currently popular "biblical" case for same-sex marriage is misguided in just about every possible way.

Digging Deeper

For most students of the Bible, this challenge is so obviously wrong it's laughable. I wouldn't waste time on it if it hadn't gained traction recently, thanks to viral online videos and a best-selling book by Matthew Vines.[3]

Vines says he believes the Bible is entirely true and authoritative. He also says the only homosexuality the Bible condemns is that which involves either excessive lust or unequal relationships. "Excessive lust" has to do with straight men being unsatisfied with their straight experiences and going roaming to add homosexual experiences to them. Unequal relationships had to do with men and boys, or sometimes men and men, where one takes the submissive "woman's" role. That was the homosexuality Paul knew about, according to Vines, so that was the homosexuality Paul condemned. But Paul had no knowledge of committed, monogamous same-sex relationships, so

---

3. Matthew Vines, *God and the Gay Christian: The Biblical Case in Support of Same-Sex Relationships* (New York: Convergent Books, 2014). Vines agrees that homosexuality was prohibited in the Old Testament; this is about the New Testament era only.

he couldn't have been talking about them. Therefore Vines concludes that God approves of same-sex marriage.

There's so much wrong with this it's hard to know where to start, but start I must, so I'll begin with two ways in which Vines is most notably wrong. For one thing, he has his historical facts wrong. In a moment we'll look at the evidence for that. For another thing, we can identify errors in his logic without even looking at the historical evidence. For example:

1. He draws a strong conclusion based on a lack of evidence. It looks like this: *I don't know of any long-term, committed, same-sex relationships in the first-century; therefore God's Word doesn't specifically condemn them; and from this I conclude that if there had been any, God's Word would have approved of them.* If that didn't make sense to you, don't worry; it shouldn't make sense. It's not good thinking. No one with any sense draws society-wrenching conclusions out of a mere lack of information—but Vines has.

2. His theory draws a conclusion from what *nobody wrote* about in the first century. ("Nobody wrote about committed, monogamous same-sex relationships, therefore Paul wasn't talking about that.") This interpretation depends on two things: (a) nobody wrote about those things, and (b) we *know* that nobody wrote about those things. Do you see how much it would take to be confident in this? There's no way we could know what *nobody* wrote without reading *everything* that *everybody* wrote. But this is absurd. No one could get the facts behind this interpretation right without reading everything anybody wrote in ancient Greece, Rome, Judea, Asia—everywhere Paul ever traveled! It's one thing to say that historical scholarship helps us understand the Bible. It's another thing to say that a biblical passage is *completely misleading* unless we know what every other first-century writer *never said* about a topic.

   In fact, this is like reestablishing the pre-Reformation doctrine that laypeople shouldn't be allowed to interpret Scripture for themselves—except it's worse than that. There was a day when only priests were allowed access to the Bible. By Vines's principle here, no one could interpret the Bible except the few Greek and Roman scholars who knew all of the surrounding literature. (And I haven't even gone into the vast quantities of literature that have been lost since then.) This is a strange and unorthodox view of God's revelation.

3. Vines's view can't afford to run into certain new discoveries. If anyone ever found out the apostle Paul knew about long-term, committed, monogamous same-sex relationships, Vines's theory would collapse. This is disturbingly similar to what many skeptics believe about the Bible: that the next new archaeological find could topple the whole thing. It's the opposite of what Christians believe: our major doctrines will stand up to any new scholarly finding that might come along. That's part of our view of Scripture, and since Vines claims to believe in the Bible, it should be part of his belief about Scripture, too. But it can't be, since his interpretation is held hostage to what scholars (hopefully) never discover.

4. It's too late, anyway. Vines is just wrong. (Here's where we draw on knowledge of ancient history to support our answer.) Paul had plenty of reason to know of committed, monogamous same-sex relationships.

Dr. Michael Brown took part in an informal radio debate with Vines in June 2014, during which this topic came up. Shortly after that debate, Dr. Brown wrote a very readable article that draws together many sources showing that Vines is mistaken. As he explains,

> There are texts that are roughly contemporaneous with the New Testament writings that speak of two men "marrying" each other or of two (adult) men being in love with each other. . . . Some of it is so powerful that it absolutely and totally sinks the entire historical argument Matthew Vines sought to make on behalf of "gay Christianity."

In the words of Anthony Thiselton, a respected scholar who wrote a 1,450-page commentary on 1 Corinthians, "Paul witnessed around him both abusive relationships of power or money and examples of 'genuine love' between males. . . . The more closely writers examine Greco-Roman society and the pluralism of its ethical traditions, the more the Corinthian situation appears to resonate with our own."

Top gay and lesbian scholars have documented this as well, as noted by professor Robert Gagnon, the foremost authority on the Bible and homosexuality.[4]

5. And finally, for centuries on end, Greek language scholars have consistently taken the relevant passages to mean that all homosexual practice is immoral. No one saw any other meaning in those passages until some people came along who had a vested interest in finding it there. For more on that, I recommend you read Michael Brown's *Can You Be Gay and Christian?*[5]

Matthew Vines claims to believe in the Bible. He also claims to be able to find support for gay marriage there. Here's what's going on instead: he *needs* to find it there in order to rationalize his chosen lifestyle. So he does—whether it's actually there or not. That's the wrong way to handle Scripture.

Tips for Talking with Your Teen

Parent, I need to advise you in advance, much of what I have to say under this topic will depend on your teen knowing what the Bible

---

4. Michael Brown, "A 'Gay Christian' Advocate Sinks His Own Ship," WND Commentary, July 2, 2014, www.wnd.com/2014/07/a-gay-christian-advocate-sinks -his-own-ship/. Also see Robert Gagnon's article, "A Book Not to Be Embraced: A Critical Review Essay on Stacy Johnson's *A Time to Embrace*," September 30, 2008, www.robgagnon.net/articles/homosexStacyJohnsonSJT2.pdf.
5. Michael L. Brown, *Can You Be Gay and Christian? Responding with Love and Truth to Questions About Homosexuality* (Lake Mary, FL: FrontLine, 2014).

really teaches and why he or she believes it's true. I have resources in the back of this book to help with that. Along with understanding how to stand strong in a pro-LGBT world, I can't think of anything that could be more important for your teen to learn. If I had space I would share with you the disturbing research showing how many teens from strong, evangelical families and churches walk away from the faith, and how many of them say they're leaving because they had questions that were never answered, or they never knew of any good reasons to believe Christianity is actually true.

I don't want to go too far off on that topic, so I'll leave it at that, hoping that short but urgent word will cause you to encourage your teen to study up on reasons to believe. Maybe your church's youth pastor can take the lead on teaching about it. At any rate, this recommendation doesn't just go with this topic—it goes with a teen's (and an adult's!) whole Christian life.

(Remember—this isn't a script.)

Son [or daughter], the first thing you need to find out when someone brings up this challenge is whether the two of you stand on common ground concerning the truth of Scripture. If the person says he believes in the Bible (as Matthew Vines says he does), then these questions might be helpful:

How do you know that Paul never knew about committed same-sex relationships? (This will help you reach common ground of a different sort: neither of you knows enough about ancient history to be able to agree knowledgeably with Vines.)

Suppose it were true that Paul had never heard about that kind of relationship. Would that mean he would have approved of it if he had known? (The answer is, it doesn't mean that at all.)

You and I believe that Paul was writing under the inspiration of the Holy Spirit. Do you think the Holy Spirit wanted us to make this hugely crucial decision based on what scholars would never find? What if they did find it?

If that doesn't communicate the point, let the person know that you have sources that show Vines is wrong anyway. I know you won't have those sources memorized, but you can always come back and get them at home. Paul knew about committed same-sex relationships. If he had wanted to make exceptions like Vines says he was making, he could have said so. If the Holy Spirit had intended to make that exception, he certainly would have. He didn't.

What if the person you're talking with doesn't believe the Bible at all, however? In that case there's probably more than one thing going on: they're criticizing the Bible, they're criticizing you for believing in the Bible, and they may even be mocking Bible-believers for disagreeing with each other over what the Bible says on this.

You don't need to debate biblical interpretation with someone who wouldn't believe the right interpretation even if he found it. Instead, you can simplify the conversation by saying something like, "Vines is wrong, and if you really want me to explain how he's wrong, I could do that (or I know a pastor who can, or my mom or dad could do it). But look, I don't even know why you're bringing it up. This is a question about what the Bible says. It's an in-house debate among people who believe in the Bible, which doesn't include you. Now, if you want to talk about whether there are good reasons to believe in the Bible, that's a completely different topic. We could do that if you like. I'll leave it up to you: where would you like to go from here?"

"You're just like the southerners who used the Bible to defend slavery."

The Challenge
"Southern slaveholders used the Bible to defend what they were doing, and what you're doing is just as wrong."

Truths Your Teen Needs to Know
Yes, white southerners used the Bible to defend slavery. That either means the Bible was wrong or that they interpreted it wrong. It's easy to tell which of those was true: they made definite, foolish mistakes in their interpretations of Scripture. They read it in a biased, self-centered, and false way. This is so obvious they should have known it at the time. The Bible's prohibitions on homosexuality are obvious enough, too, for us to be able to see what's really there. The Bible wasn't unclear on slavery being wrong the way it was done in the South, and it isn't unclear on homosexuality being wrong now.

Digging Deeper
Some pre–Civil War southerners used the Bible to defend their slaveholding ways. When they did that, the Bible wasn't wrong, they were. They were doing what a lot of people do when they want their religion to support their sin: they convinced themselves the Bible said it was okay, even though it clearly never said that.

Now, I do need to admit that the Bible condoned a certain sort of slavery that existed in its day. I'll admit, too, that's hard to understand today. The explanation lies in complex cultural, economic, and political differences between the world of the Bible and today's world, and especially in huge differences between slavery then (often more like indentured servanthood) and slavery as we think of it today. To explain all that is beyond the scope of this book. (Glenn Sunshine wrote a helpful chapter on it in *True Reason: Confronting the Irrationality of the New Atheism*.)[6]

---

6. "Christianity and Slavery," in *True Reason: Confronting the Irrationality of the New Atheism*, ed. Tom Gilson and Carson Weitnauer (Grand Rapids: Kregel, 2014), 287–302.

In short, slavery (servanthood) in the Bible was completely different from slavery in the South. Southern slavery seriously violated multiple clearly stated biblical principles. The Bible clearly prohibits kidnapping for slavery and the slave trade in general (Exod. 21:16; 1 Tim. 1:10). Ephesians 6:1–9 instructs masters to treat slaves according to the way they would want to be treated themselves. From that much alone, it's plain to see that southerners who used the Bible to justify their form of slavery were wrong—obviously wrong.

And this isn't advanced Bible interpretation. It's right there on the surface. The Bible's commands against southern-style slavery are clear enough for anyone to see. The people who practiced it had every reason to know they were committing a gross violation of Scripture.

And the Bible's commands against homosexual practice are just as plain, clear, and obvious as its prohibitions against southern-style slavery.

We're not making the same mistake southern slaveholders made. They violated clear and obvious commands of Scripture. We're *not* violating any clear and obvious commands of Scripture. We're following its commands instead.

If we were actually making a southern-slavery sort of mistake, it should be obvious to see how we're getting Scripture wrong, just as it should have been obvious to slaveholders that they were getting the Bible wrong—if only they had paid attention. It isn't. On the contrary, it's easy to see throughout the Bible that marriage is for a man and a woman, which settles the gay marriage issue from a biblical perspective. It's also easy to see that sexual activity is only for married persons. That settles the rest of the issue. The Bible affirms sexual relationships between husband and wife, and husband and wife *only*.

A challenger could come back to ask about additional instructions from the Bible he still thinks we're violating—for example, that we're violating the Golden Rule by not treating LGBT people the way we would want to be treated. He might say there's something deeply unloving about discriminating against LGBT people, and that we're disobeying God's Word on that count.

If we were actually harming people by what we were doing, we would indeed be in violation of Scripture, but there's nothing inherently harmful, unloving, or damaging about believing and speaking the truth about God's moral standards. I explain this in greater detail in chapter 5, and also under the topic, "If God is love, why would he be opposed to committed, loving relationships?"

Now, all of the above is for people who believe in the Bible (or at least say they do) and think we're getting it wrong. Sometimes, though, this charge comes from people who don't care how accurate our interpretations are; they're saying the Bible itself is wrong.

That opens up a whole new set of questions and answers, most of which are beyond the scope of this book, but I'll mention one that does fit in with this book's overall theme. The person might be thinking, *If the Bible teaches that slavery is okay, then the Bible must be wrong; and if the Bible teaches that homosexuality is bad, then the Bible must be wrong on that account, too.* In other words, if the Bible got one thing so obviously wrong, we shouldn't trust it on anything.

As I said, though, the Bible never teaches that slavery is okay *the way people today think of slavery.* It teaches the exact opposite of that. So that clears the Bible of guilt on the first part of that charge. As for the second part, this whole book explains reasons to believe the Bible is both good *and* true when it speaks about sexual morality.

If you need further background on the slavery question, I suggest you read the chapter in *True Reason* that I've already mentioned. For even more information, refer to Paul Copan's excellent book, *Is God a Moral Monster?: Making Sense of the Old Testament God.*[7]

Tips for Talking with Your Teen

You might say something like this to your teen, always bearing in mind that this isn't a script; it's a guide for discussion:

The way to deal with this really depends on where the question is coming from. Is the questioner challenging your interpretation of Scripture, or is

---

7. Paul Copan, *Is God a Moral Monster?: Making Sense of the Old Testament God* (Grand Rapids: Baker, 2011).

he challenging the truth of Scripture itself? The simple way to find out is just by asking him.

If he believes the Bible is true but you're interpreting it wrong, your answer should be fairly easy. Open up the Bible to Exodus 21:16, 1 Timothy 1:10, and Ephesians 6:5–9, and help him see how plainly wrong the southern slaveholders were. Explain how easy it would have been to show them the same thing in their day. There's no getting around the fact that they were obviously wrong.

Once you've gone that far, ask him whether he can show you just as easily that your views about sexuality are wrong today, according to the Bible. He won't be able to do it: it's impossible. Matthew Vines's approach is hardly that clear! (See the topic just prior to this one.) Then walk him through the passages that show how clear the Bible is regarding marriage and morality.

It's well worth it to show him we're not making any obvious errors concerning homosexuality, the way southerners made obvious mistakes concerning slavery. So whatever mistakes we might be making (and face it: we're human, so we could be making some) we're not making the same kind of mistake they made. The two can't fairly be compared.

What about the person who thinks the Bible is wrong? Again, try explaining to him that we're not making the same kind of mistake the southern slaveholders made. Remember, though, that you would only be answering part of the question. You'll want to ask, "Does that answer your question, or do you have something further you're wondering about?"

Whichever form the challenge takes, if you don't have the answer right on the tip of your tongue, I suggest you ask the other person to give you a bit of time to look up your sources. Take the time you need to study and learn, and then go back to him when you can to continue the conversation.

AFTERWORD

These are unfamiliar waters we're navigating these days. Over the history of Christianity and around the world today, hostility, persecution, and other challenges have been normal. Not so in the United States, at least, not until recently. Times are changing.

As parents we must prepare our children for the kind of world they will face—a world we've never had to face ourselves. We can't ignore the rapid changes in our culture, and how those changes are affecting the way Christianity is viewed. This morning as I write this, I'm reading a *Daily Beast* column by Sally Kohn, who says, "Will anti-gay Christians be politically and socially ostracized? I sure hope so."[1]

But we still want our children to grow up in the fullness of the life of Christ. With that in mind, we can't just abdicate our teens' spiritual preparation to the Internet, to their schools, or even to our churches. Yes, the church is crucial, but parents are even more so.

Gay-rights advocates are good at putting Christianity in a negative light. The reality is very different from that: God is good, Jesus Christ is good, and the way of Christ is good, even when it involves moral prohibitions. Your children won't hear that truth from the world. They won't necessarily hear it even from your church, since many churches shy away from these hard questions. They need your help with it. They don't need you to be an expert; they just need you

---

1. Sally Kohn, "The New Post-Homophobic Christianity," *The Daily Beast,* July 5, 2015, www.thedailybeast.com/articles/2015/07/05/the-new-post-homophobic -christianity.html.

to work through the questions with them. I trust and I pray that this book will prove to be a useful guide for you as you spend that time with them.

I trust, too, that you will support your children with prayer as they move into a different kind of world than you and I first entered as young adults. Their Christianity will not be popular; in fact, it may even come under strong attack. (Yours and mine might, too.) Jesus Christ is strong enough to bear them up, though, and his truth is powerful enough to endure through all challenges. As his Word tells us in 1 Peter 4:12–19:

> Beloved, do not be surprised at the fiery trial when it comes upon you to test you, as though something strange were happening to you. But rejoice insofar as you share Christ's sufferings, that you may also rejoice and be glad when his glory is revealed. If you are insulted for the name of Christ, you are blessed, because the Spirit of glory and of God rests upon you. But let none of you suffer as a murderer or a thief or an evildoer or as a meddler. Yet if anyone suffers as a Christian, let him not be ashamed, but let him glorify God in that name. For it is time for judgment to begin at the household of God; and if it begins with us, what will be the outcome for those who do not obey the gospel of God? And "If the righteous is scarcely saved, what will become of the ungodly and the sinner?" Therefore let those who suffer according to God's will entrust their souls to a faithful Creator while doing good.

Face the questions squarely. Seek the truth. God will guide you. Stand with the truth. Help your teens stand with the truth. God will stand with you in it.

A VISION FOR MARRIAGE IN OUR CULTURE: TEN ESSENTIALS

As important as it is to equip our children to stand strong in the face of LGBT activism, it's just as important that we do everything we can to recover a godly vision of marriage in our culture. Here I propose a vision for victory on marriage, in the form of ten essentials.

Note that I do not say "victory on *gay* marriage." The issue is deeper and larger than that. It's about all marriage. I'm also not framing this as "ten steps to victory" or any such thing. It's not a formula. It's a picture, a vision.

Some of these essentials have to do with study and communication, some with building loving and genuine relationships. There isn't an easy item anywhere on this list. If I'm right in thinking that all ten of them are essential, we have a lot of hard work to do.

What will it take to recover marriage in our culture?

1. Reframe what we're seeking. Our real challenge isn't to stand against same-sex marriage; it's to build and support marriage in its strong and true form.
2. Recover a true understanding of marriage, particularly among

Adapted from "A Vision for Marriage in Our Culture: Ten Essentials," June 5, 2012, www.thinkingchristian.net/posts/2012/06/a-vision-for-marriage-in-our -culture-ten-essentials/.

those of us who support male–female marriage. Marriage is greater and deeper than just the happy pairing of a man and a woman. It's also the basis of child-rearing (generation) and helping build our children and communities for our children's children (re-generation). It's the center of family and the foundation of a stable society. It's a reflection of the relationship between Christ and his people.

Heterosexual couples tragically led the way in making marriage merely about happiness together, and also in making it optional for sexual expression. Why should anyone be surprised that same-sex couples have followed? It was the fruit of our own error. It ought to have been predictable.

3. Rediscover and relocate the source and grounding of marriage. It's not in "traditional values." That phrasing leaves me cold, frankly. It's bland and empty; it makes an idol of the past without giving sufficient thought to what was good about it—and what wasn't. Real marriage, in contrast, connects directly and timelessly to the essence of humanness, family, community, and culture.

4. Train ourselves to be able to articulate the truth about marriage, in persuasive terms transcending the usual slogans and images. This will take study and patience, for it requires conversing at a level of reasoned discourse that few people in our culture are accustomed to—but the stakes are too high to shrug it off just because it's a tough challenge.

5. Equip ourselves to explain why standing in favor of marriage is neither hatred nor phobia. Same-sex marriage advocates have framed our position that way, without caring to notice that not everyone they describe that way actually is hateful or phobic. Some are, certainly, but it's far from universal. This is a matter for explanation, demonstration, and persuasion.

6. Reject spiritual pride, which is loathsome to everyone, especially to God. While it is right to agree that what's wrong is wrong, it is never right to imply spiritual superiority.

7. Show genuine and continuing love toward gays, lesbians, bisex-

uals, and transsexuals. This is not to be confused with agreement or acquiescence with their program. To support falsehood is not to act in love. The point rather is to be genuine, to be willing to connect in authentic relationships—to be friends.

Note that there is an unavoidable asymmetry connected to both 6 and 7. Gay advocacy leaders can (and do) proclaim loudly that we are hateful and phobic, but it's impossible to love loudly. We can only do it personally. They like to make us out to be arrogant, too, which is also hard to answer with a quick press release! Public remedial apologies and confessions of error are too easily tainted with the whiff of manipulation, which is much more easily dispelled in the close-up context of real relationships.

Our individual friendships with gays and lesbians may not much affect the grand inclusive stereotype some want to impose upon us. Still it's right to do the right thing, for the sake of integrity if nothing else.

8. Engage productively in the campaign to recover the true definition of marriage. The June 2015 Supreme Court decision has set us back in our effort to teach and practice what is true about marriage. We cannot be content with the current state of legal affairs. Sure, our strategies must be different now than they formerly were; but just as *Roe v. Wade* wasn't the last word on abortion, *Obergefell v. Hodges* need not be the last word on same-sex marriage.

9. Rebuild a culture of marriage, where a couple's mutual love and relationship are not the whole point, but where family and community are deeply intertwined in it right from the start. (Christian couples also know that God belongs at the center with them, between them, and holding them together.) This means that those who are married stay married. It means we stay with it even when it's hard, as it is for every couple at times, and that we get the help we need when it's beyond us.

10. Last but really first: Suffuse all these efforts with prayer, for this is a spiritual vision and not just a natural one.

I don't want to understate the challenge of any of this—especially item 9, for some couples. Again, I didn't say any of this was going to be easy. For the sake of our future, though, and especially our children's future, none of it is optional.

I believe it's a vision worth pursuing.

RESOURCE GUIDE

You and Your Teenager

Powell, Kara E., and Chap Clark. *Sticky Faith: Everyday Ideas to Build Lasting Faith in Your Kids.* Grand Rapids: Zondervan, 2011.
This extremely practical yet highly informed book is the best one I know of for helping parents understand how to build their children's faith to last.

Smith, Christian, and Melanie Lundquist Denton. *Soul Searching: The Religious and Spiritual Lives of American Teenagers.* New York: Oxford University Press, 2005.
Smith, Christian, and Patricia Snell. *Souls in Transition: The Religious and Spiritual Lives of Emerging Adults.* New York: Oxford University Press, 2009.
Somewhat academic yet readable, this pair of books presents the best research yet on the spirituality of American teens and young adults. If you want to know the general trends for religion in these age ranges, this is the place to look. (A companion website, youthandreligion.nd.edu, gives immediate free access to some of the same information.)

Kinnaman, David, and Aly Hawkins. *You Lost Me: Why Young Christians Are Leaving Church . . . and Rethinking Faith.* Grand Rapids: Baker, 2011.
You Lost Me is a product of the Barna Research Group, of which David Kinnaman is president. It provides a quicker, more readable version of research into why young people abandon church and faith.

McFarland, Alex. *The 21 Toughest Questions Your Kids Will Ask About Christianity: And How to Answer Them Confidently*. A Focus on the Family book. Reprint edition. Carol Stream, IL: Tyndale, 2013. Like part 3 of the book you now hold in your hands—though covering more territory than just homosexuality—*The 21 Toughest Questions* is designed to give practical assistance to parents who need help answering hard questions.

Marriage and Morality: Christian/Conservative Views

Books and Articles

Brown, Michael L. *A Queer Thing Happened to America: And What a Long Strange Trip It's Been*. Concord, NC: EqualTime Books, 2011.

Brown, Michael L. *Can You Be Gay and Christian?: Responding with Love and Truth to Questions About Homosexuality*. Lake Mary, FL: FrontLine, 2014.

Michael Brown is an accomplished Old Testament scholar who has spent many hours lovingly interacting with the LGBT community, and has also explained for Christian readers some of the strange and disturbing history of the gay-rights movement (*A Queer Thing*), and why the Bible does not support homosexuality (*Can You Be Gay and Christian?*).

Esolen, Anthony. *Defending Marriage: Twelve Arguments for Sanity*. Charlotte, NC: Saint Benedict Press, 2014.

Esolen, Anthony. "Sanity & Matrimony: Ten Arguments in Defense of Marriage (Part 1 of 2)." *Touchstone*, July/August 2010, www.touchstonemag.com/archives/article.php?id=23-04-028-f.

"Sanity & Matrimony: Ten Arguments in Defense of Marriage (Part 2 of 2)." *Touchstone*, September/October 2010, www.touchstonemag.com/archives/article.php?id=23-05-025-f.

The ten arguments of "Sanity & Matrimony" comprise the most brilliant brief explanation I've seen for why man-and-woman is the only right form of marriage. Esolen expanded them and added two more to produce the equally outstanding book *Defending Marriage*.

Feldhahn, Shaunti. *The Good News About Marriage: Debunking Discouraging Myths About Marriage and Divorce.* Sisters, OR: Multnomah, 2014.

Recent, readable, surprising research into the true health of marriage in our culture.

Gagnon, Robert. "A Book Not to Be Embraced: A Critical Review Essay on Stacy Johnson's *A Time to Embrace.*" September 30, 2008. www.robgagnon.net/articles/homosexStacyJohnsonSJT2.pdf.

Dr. Gagnon is a leading researcher on sexuality and the Bible, and this article is a good example of his work. See also the follow-up at www.robgagnon.net/articles/homosexStacyJohnsonMoreReasonsCritique.pdf.

Girgis, Sherif, Ryan T. Anderson, and Robert George. *What Is Marriage? Man and Woman: A Defense.* New York: Encounter Books, 2012.

Girgis, Sherif, Robert George, and Ryan T. Anderson. "What Is Marriage?" *Harvard Journal of Law and Public Policy* 34, no. 1 (2010). www.harvard-jlpp.com/wp-content/uploads/2013/10/George Final.pdf.

These two resources, sharing the same three authors and nearly the same name, remain the best philosophical defenses yet written for natural (man–woman) marriage. I suggest you begin with the *Harvard Journal* article, since it's shorter and it's available for free, then move on to the book. Both of these are somewhat more academically written than most of the other resources I'm recommending here. They are worth the effort. Christians need to be able to understand and speak to what these authors have presented.

Gagnon, Robert. *The Bible and Homosexual Practice: Texts and Hermeneutics.* Nashville: Abingdon Press, 2002.

The definitive academic work on the subject.

Marin, Andrew. *Love Is an Orientation: Elevating the Conversation with the Gay Community.* Downers Grove, IL: IVP Books, 2009.

Andrew Marin is an evangelical Christian who understands how to connect with God's grace across the divide toward the homosexual community. I recommend this book highly for its gracious, thoughtful understanding of the LGBT experience from an outsider's perspective. (For accurate biblical interpretation, you would want to study the books by Brown, McDowell and Stonestreet, or Gagnon instead.)

McDowell, Sean, and John Stonestreet. *Same-Sex Marriage: A Thoughtful Approach to God's Design for Marriage.* Ventura, CA: Regal Books, 2014.

For a readable yet strong explanation of marriage and why it matters, I recommend you begin with this book by Sean McDowell and John Stonestreet. Not only do they explain what marriage is and why it matters, they also show what you and I can realistically do to keep supporting marriage even as our culture keeps trying to undermine it.

Reilly, Robert R. *Making Gay Okay: How Rationalizing Homosexual Behavior Is Changing Everything.* San Francisco: Ignatius Press, 2014.

This book bridges the purposes fulfilled earlier by *What Is Marriage* and *A Queer Thing Happened to America.* It's a philosophical defense of marriage coupled with a fascinating historical overview of how we found ourselves so quickly in a culture that won't support real marriage.

Websites

Robert Gagnon, http://www.robgagnon.net

While his tone is sometimes more confrontational than I prefer, Robert Gagnon is the go-to resource for factual information on marriage, morality, and the Bible, specifically on topics relating to homosexuality.

First Things, www.firstthings.com

First Things is published by the Institute on Religion and Public Life, an interreligious, nonpartisan research and educational 501(c)(3) organization. It is one of the most consistently thoughtful magazines around today, with a strong pro-marriage perspective.

The Stream, www.stream.org
The Stream is the highest quality website I know of for trustworthy information and insightful Christian perspectives on a wide spectrum of social and cultural matters. This includes, of course, marriage and homosexuality. I joined the staff of *The Stream* as senior editor and ministry coordinator just before final edits were completed on *Critical Conversations.* I do not consider it a high quality website because I've joined it; in fact, the reverse is true: I jumped at the opportunity to join because I consider it such a high quality website.

Touchstone, www.touchstonemag.com
As "A Journal of Mere Christianity," *Touchstone* provides a place where Christians of various backgrounds can speak on the basis of shared belief. Consistently thoughtful, it too has a strong pro-marriage perspective.

Marriage and Morality: Pro-LGBT Views

If you care to survey some pro-LGBT thinking from the original sources, these are good places to start: disturbing, yet informative.

Kirk, Marshall, and Hunter Madsen. *After the Ball: How America Will Conquer Its Fear and Hatred of Gays in the 90's.* New York: Plume, 1990.

Kirk, Marshall K., and Erastes Pill. "The Overhauling of Straight America." *Guide* (November 1987). library.gayhomeland.org /0018/EN/EN_Overhauling_Straight.htm.

Vines, Matthew. *God and the Gay Christian: The Biblical Case in Support of Same-Sex Relationships.* New York: Convergent Books, 2014.

Christianity and Truth

The remaining items in this resource guide are all on the general topic of Christian apologetics. *Apologetics* (from the Greek word *apologia* in 1 Peter 3:15 meaning "answer" or "defense") is the study of reasons for confidence in the truth of Christianity. Teens need to know that the faith we're teaching them is more than just our opinion—especially when they're coming under fire for taking a Christian stand on marriage and morality. Christianity is based in real history and it's supported by good evidence.

There are too many great books on apologetics for me to include a significant number of them. Here are a few of my favorites, ranked (by my subjective opinion) according to readability: from more readable to more challenging. The first ten or so are all highly readable. Even though I've kept the list fairly short, it might still be hard to know where to begin, so I've marked a few of these books as "*This is where to start . . ."

McDowell, Josh, and Sean McDowell. *More Than a Carpenter.* Revised. Carol Stream, IL: Tyndale, 2011. *This is where to start for the quickest, easiest read on how we know the faith is true.

McDowell, Josh, and Sean McDowell. *The Unshakable Truth: How You Can Experience the 12 Essentials of a Relevant Faith.* Eugene, OR: Harvest House, 2010.

McDowell, Josh, and Dave Sterrett. *Is the Bible True . . . Really?: A Dialogue on Skepticism, Evidence, and Truth.* The Coffee House Chronicles. Chicago: Moody Publishers, 2010.

Sherrard, Michael C. *Relational Apologetics: Defending the Christian Faith with Holiness, Respect, and Truth.* Second edition. Grand Rapids: Kregel, 2015.

Wallace, J. Warner. *Cold-Case Christianity: A Homicide Detective Investigates the Claims of the Gospels.* Colorado Springs: David C. Cook, 2013. *This is where to start for the best readable comprehensive look at Christian apologetics.

Koukl, Gregory. *Tactics: A Game Plan for Discussing Your Christian Convictions.* Grand Rapids: Zondervan, 2009. *This is where to start for the best introduction into speaking your convictions without having to be an expert.

Mittelberg, Mark. *The Questions Christians Hope No One Will Ask: (With Answers).* Carol Stream: IL: Tyndale, 2010.

Geisler, Norman L., and Frank Turek. *I Don't Have Enough Faith to Be an Atheist.* Wheaton, IL: Crossway, 2004.

Russell, Jeffrey Burton. *Exposing Myths About Christianity: A Guide* *to Answering 145 Viral Lies and Legends.* Downers Grove, IL: IVP Books, 2012. *This is where to start for quick answers to many more slogans like the ones I addressed in part 3, on a much broader range of topics.

Lamb, David T. *God Behaving Badly: Is the God of the Old Testament Angry, Sexist and Racist?* Downers Grove, IL: IVP Books, 2011. *This is where to start for answers to the charge that the God of the Bible is intrinsically evil.

The list gets somewhat more challenging from here:

Keller, Timothy. *The Reason for God: Belief in an Age of Skepticism.* New York: Dutton, 2008. *This is where to start for the most pastorally aware, human-sensitive approach to apologetics I know of.

Craig, William Lane. *Reasonable Faith: Christian Truth and Apologetics.* Wheaton, IL: Crossway, 2008. This is not where to start. It's where to land. It's a great work of Christian apologetics for those who have the interest and capacity to follow a more challenging piece of writing.

Apologetics Websites

Thinking Christian, www.thinkingchristian.net
My own blog, covering a broad range of topics on Christianity and culture.

Natasha Crain: Inspiration for Intentional Christian Parenting, www.christianmomthoughts.com
Outstanding parent-oriented discussions on the truth and meaning of Christianity in contemporary culture.

Stand to Reason, www.str.org
The one website I most recommend for finding quick, solid answers to almost any question concerning the truth of Christianity.

Christian Apologetics Alliance, www.christianapologeticsalliance.com
The public face of the Christian Apologetics Alliance Facebook group, with hordes of articles on every apologetics-related topic.

Ratio Christi, www.ratiochristi.org
Ratio Christi is a nationwide student apologetics alliance with a presence
on college campuses across the country. This website is much more than an
explanation and introduction to the ministry—it's also a gathering place for
information and articles on speakers, events, authors, and articles across the
whole community of apologetics.

Reasonable Faith, www.reasonablefaith.org
The web home of William Lane Craig, one of the leading apologetics think-
ers in the world today, and, like str.org (though on a more challenging level),
a great place to look up specific answers to a broad range of questions.

Ravi Zacharias International Ministries, www.rzim.org
A third website with answers to your questions. I would judge it to fall
between str.org and reasonablefaith.org in its readability and intellectual
challenge.

Other Books by Tom Gilson

Finally, if you have found *Critical Conversations* to be helpful, I invite
you to look into my other books. Both of these would land at about
the middle of the readability scale.

Gilson, Tom, and Carson Weitnauer, eds. *True Reason: Confronting the
Irrationality of the New Atheism.* Grand Rapids: Kregel, 2014.
A collection of essays challenging New Atheist claims that atheism is the one
way to live and think reasonably.

Gilson, Tom. *Peter Boghossian, Atheist Tactician: A Preliminary Response
to* A Manual for Creating Atheists. Self-published ebook, 2013.
Available via www.thinkingchristian.net.
This is a response to a direct challenge raised by an atheist professor who
wants to help people everywhere create more atheists.